emergence

Books by Barbara Marx Hubbard

Conscious Evolution: Awakening the Power of Our Social Potential

The Hunger of Eve: One Woman's Odyssey Toward the Future

The Revelation: A Message of Hope for the New Millennium

The Evolutionary Journey

emergence
The Shift from Ego to Essence

Barbara Marx Hubbard

WALSCH
W
BOOKS

an imprint of
HAMPTON ROADS
PUBLISHING COMPANY, INC.
www.hrpub.com

Cover design by Marjoram Productions
Cover art by Teresa Collins

For information write:
Hampton Roads Publishing Company, Inc.
1125 Stoney Ridge Road
Charlottesville, VA 22902

Or call: 804-296-2772
Fax: 804-296-5096
e-mail: hrpc@hrpub.com
www.hrpub.com

If you are unable to order this book from your local
bookseller, you may order directly from the publisher.
Call 1-800-766-8009, toll-free.

Library of Congress Catalog Card Number: 00-111237

ISBN 1-57174-204-2

10 9 8 7 6 5 4 3 2 1

Printed on acid-free paper in the United States

DEDICATION

Emergence is dedicated to my eldest daughter, Suzanne. Several years ago, she asked me a critical question: "What do we know about the developmental path of the Universal Human?" We began to search together to discover the pattern of our own emergence. How did it happen that each of us had evolved so far beyond the worldview and state of being in which we were born? We probed our own life paths, sharing our earliest memories, our unitive experiences, our woundings, choices, awakenings, and passionate desire to more fully express our unique creativity through joining with each other. Then Suzanne, a weaver, mother, and gardener, set to work to discover a "Blueprint," a new lens that served as a portal for us to discover the actual process of our own personal emergence. She began to write *The Life Book* which lays out the Blueprint.

Meanwhile, I continued to discover the pattern of my own and others' emergence as a new type of human, one that has been gestating in the psyche of humanity for thousands of years and only now is coming forth en masse as a new norm. Key elements of Suzanne's *Life Book* "Blueprint," a work-in-progress, is reprinted on page 183, so that the reader can also see a portal through which this way of conscious self-evolution begins.

Emergence is dedicated to Sidney Thomas Lanier, whose faith in the emergence of the "sovereign person" in each of us, and his love of me for the past ten years of learning, has drawn me forth, preparing me to enter the mysterious process of becoming a "cosmic coupling."

Emergence is also dedicated to all my beloved children: Woodleigh Marx Hubbard, an inspired children's illustrator and champion of children's innocence and joy; Alexandra Morton, whale researcher in British Columbia, passionate environmentalist, and champion of interspecies co-existence; Wade Hubbard, a musician and entrepreneur who, with his wife, Kehau, is setting the scene to bring the great power of popular music to illuminate the new story; and Maj. Lloyd Frost Hubbard and his wife, Laura, who bring to the Air Force and to flying the spiritual commitment of love and excellence.

Also, to my beloved sister Patricia Ellsberg, my best friend for the past fifty years, who through ACE (Association for Cooperative Economics) is pioneering in how to redirect consumer spending for the support of organizations now serving the Earth. And to my sister Jacqueline Barnett, an artist and source of ever-ready strength, wisdom, and inspiration to me.

To the "Seed Group" of Santa Barbara, who invited me into the resonant field that launched the repatterning of my life, and the coming into form of my visionary work; with special thanks to Teresa Collins and Marshall Lefferts, co-directors of the Foundation for Conscious Evolution; and to Anne Milgrim, Patricia Gaul, and Jai Jamison, who are contributing so much to the work.

To Carolyn Anderson and John Zwerver, who pioneered with me the core group process and who are now creating *The Co-creator's Handbook: an Experiential Guide for Discovering and Fulfilling Your Soul's Purpose.*

To Nancy Carroll, who brought the Foundation through its early years to its readiness to grow.

To my editor, Nancy Marriott, without whose help I could not have finished this book.

To my benefactor, Laurance S. Rockefeller, who supported this work for ten years, bringing it to this point of fulfillment.

To Neale Donald Walsch, who is giving to millions the courage to bring God home within us all.

A Greater Evolution is
the Real Goal of Humanity

"The coming of a spiritual age must be preceded by the appearance of an increasing number of individuals who are no longer satisfied with the normal intellectual, vital, and physical existence of man, but perceive that a greater evolution is the real goal of humanity and attempt to effect it in themselves, to lead others to it, and to make it the recognized goal of the race. In proportion as they succeed and to the degree to which they carry this evolution, the yet unrealized potentiality which they represent will become an actual possibility of the future."

—*Sri Aurobindo*

"Find me somebody who has detached his emotional and psychological ego from the real self, without having to deny the place it plays in the scheme of things and without slaying any part of himself because the transcendence is there also, and I will have discovered the ineffable in the individual and a direct pathway for the communion of my own soul."

—*Ernest Holmes*

"There is emerging from out of the mist of myth, religious and scientific, a new thought, so new, so ancient. This thought is that the transcendent God of History indwells each of us as us. Our relation to all avatars is that of younger siblings, sisters and brothers who are awakening at last to the awesome and exhilarating truth, the final fact of the ultimate covenant. We are the heirs, the operative expressions of divinity Itself, now!"

—*Sidney Thomas Lanier*

"There are fifty million people in the United States alone that have undergone a comprehensive shift in their world-view, values, and way of life. They express serious ecological and planetary perspectives, emphasis on relationships and women's point of view, commitment to spirituality and psychological development, disaffection with the large institutions of modern life, including both left and right in politics, and rejection of materialism and status display. This is twenty-six percent of the adult population of the United States. As recently as the early 1960s, less than five percent of the population was engaged in making these momentous changes. A similar phenomenon is happening in Europe."

—*Paul H. Ray, Ph.D., and Sherry Ruth Anderson, Ph.D.*

TABLE OF CONTENTS

FOREWORD

Joseph Campbell, the great mythologist, once said that the greatest truths of the human community are best conveyed by means of stories. Although Barbara Marx Hubbard has excelled in a variety of different roles (mother, futurist, social prophet), at core she says that she is fundamentally a storyteller. But, unlike most storytellers, who content themselves with a more restricted focus, Hubbard takes as her canvas what she calls the *Whole Story of Creation*—starting with the Big Bang, moving through the emergence of physical matter, chemical interactions, biological life, and (very recently from a galactic perspective) human societies—a story that finds its ending with a new beginning involving the emergence of a new type of evolutionary human, which she calls *Homo universalis*. Central to this story line are core questions dealing with what it means to be fully human and what we need to do to best pursue this transcendental goal.

A second of Joseph Campbell's great insights also helps to describe Barbara Marx Hubbard and what her latest book, *Emergence*, is all about. In his classic work, *Hero With a Thousand Faces* (1968), Campbell describes how the essential defining ingredient of the hero is the unwillingness to accept what no longer works for oneself and others, coupled with the courage and ability to search beyond the pale to find new answers that cannot be found within the box of conventional thinking about reality. Whether or not you agree with all of the story that Hubbard continues to expand in each of her various books, keynote speeches, and workshops, I think that no one who seriously considers her work can deny that here is a genuine hero—and one whose message about consciousness and conscious evolution is uniquely appropriate for our time. Viewed from this perspective, Barbara Marx Hubbard's work can be seen as following in the great tradition of such visionary works as R.M. Bucke's *Cosmic Consciousness* (1974), P. Teilhard de Chardin's *The Phenomenon of Man* (1975), and even Deepak Chopra's most recent offering, *How to Know God* (2000).

My view of this book is strongly shaped by the fact that almost three decades ago I had the privilege of working with Joseph Campbell, Willis Harman, Duane Elgin, and others at the Stanford Research Institute (now SRI International), and Wink Franklin at the Kettering Foundation, in the preparation of a research study subsequently published as "Changing Images of Man." Although "Changing Images" received very little public attention, various pioneering thinkers like Barbara Marx Hubbard say the SRI study was a pivotal influence on their thinking about consciousness and the future. What was it about the "Changing Images" report that led Barbara to honor it by asking me to mention it in this introduction? And why is it now clear that the "torch" of conscious evolution so dimly envisioned at SRI some twenty-seven years ago is burning even more brightly today as we face a new millennium?

"Changing Images" was the first formal research study to apply Thomas S. Kuhn's (then) new theory about paradigm change to an entire society, rather than just a scientific discipline. But more than that, our study attempted to reach beyond the rational/analytic conceptual and methodological "box" of the dominant paradigm: We strove to use a balance of rational and intuitive modes of awareness in exploring how advances in human consciousness might make it possible to achieve what nowadays is called a sustainable, humane future. (Then we simply called it a "workable future.") The study concluded that an evolutionary transformation of society was needed if the increasingly turbulent waters ahead are to be navigated successfully, and that a future image or vision of humankind capable of helping facilitate that transformation would at a minimum:

- convey a holistic sense of perspective or understanding of life,
- entail an ecological ethic, emphasizing the total community of life-in-nature and the oneness of the human race,
- entail a self-realization ethic, placing the highest value on development of selfhood and declaring that an appropriate function of all social institutions is the fostering of human development,
- be multi-leveled, multi-faceted, and integrative, accommodating various cultural and personality types,
- involve balancing and coordination of satisfactions along many dimensions
- rather than the maximizing of concerns along one narrowly defined dimension, and
- be experimental, open-ended, and evolutionary.

As the discerning reader will see, Barbara Marx Hubbard's new book, *Emergence*, represents something of a continuation or completion of her prior book, *Conscious Evolution: Awakening the Power of Our Social Potential*, by way of fulfilling each of the preceding characteristics. However, whereas her earlier books dealt with the macro level—the big picture of physical, biological, and cultural evolution—*Emergence* deals with the micro level of individual human evolution. This book is essentially the autobiographical story of how Hubbard, after having a number of remarkable mystical experiences (such as are documented in *The Revelation: Our Crisis is a Birth*), found that periodic "re-connection" experiences with divine guidance are simply not enough. In order to fully integrate and unify the various aspects of one's egoic, "local" self with the essential, core, or Universal Self, a more consciously continuous relationship is needed. The specific steps that Hubbard found useful as she went about establishing this continuing relationship in consciousness are the "meat and potatoes" of this book. There are, of course, many guides and many guidebooks for doing this most challenging and rewarding of tasks, but few do so with the uniquely evolutionary slant that Barbara Marx Hubbard brings to all of her work.

There are a number of features of Hubbard's work that should be of interest, both to pioneering lay people and to intellectual, religious, and political thought leaders interested in helping to guide humanity into a peaceful and "safe" future. Her new image of our evolutionary destiny is based in part on a changing image of evolution itself. Her vision specifically includes the image of conscious evolution as a way to bridge the divide between creationism and materialism by discovering in nature an implicate order, a tendency toward higher consciousness and greater freedom through more complex order. This can be seen as the "prime directive": an in-built (naturally divine/divinely natural) designing intelligence underlying the evolution of what we call reality at all stages of emergence since the Big Bang, and especially now—a time in which we and our planet have the possibility of realizing that "our crisis is a birth."

Emergence applies this new definition of evolution to the emergence of a new person, who embodies qualities discovered to be intrinsic to the holonomic nature of the universe itself, such as non-locality, self-creation, etc. In this new person the manifested form of the prime directive, which used to be experienced outside as God, Christ, higher beings, avatars, etc., is internally experienced as our own Essential Self—universally connected to all that is—with whom we become a conscious co-creator. Rather than going straight to God as a way to transcend the ego, as was the paramount goal of traditional mystics, the emergence goal in Hubbard's life and work is co-creation with the prime directive God-ness within—personally, interpersonally, technologically, globally, universally.

This new human, enhanced by an enriched scientific, technological, and cultural noosphere, is a new being: After full emergence, our internal cosmos is no longer experienced as ego-centric, but transpersonal, just as (after Copernicus), the image of our outer cosmos went from being earth-centered to being sun-centered, and may at some future time (when interstellar space travel has become commonplace), be galaxy-centered and even universe-centered in orientation. *Emergence* thus goes beyond transpersonal psychology, seeing a species metamorphosis, placing human evolution in the context of radical new scientific, technological, and spiritual tools and capacities that are both radical and conservative as we look ahead to the new millennium: radical in the sense of cutting to the quick of technological breakthroughs (such as nanotechnology, virtual reality, and zero-point/quantum effects phenomena) and conservative in the sense of preserving and honoring the highest values and wisdom traditions of human history (e.g., the Perennial Philosophy, the Golden Rule). The almost imperceptible shift of identity from ego to essence now occurring in so many of us is a harbinger of a quantum jump to come, if and when humanity lives through this most critical period, learns ethical evolution, and begins to apply the new technological powers in an earth/space or universal environment. Phenomena such as clairvoyance, remote viewing, prayer-based healing at a distance, and other "non-local" consciousness and/or spiritual technologies—currently seen by science as for the most part anomalous, but increasingly being studied and understood—could become acceptable because for the first time they would fit the paradigm of society.

Emergence charts stages in the developmental path of this emerging human, with personal experiences, practices, and guidelines for our own emergence. And for Barbara Marx Hubbard, *Emergence* uses the threat of extinction as an ultimate evolutionary driver for the awakening of millions to transformational birth of a universal human and a universal humanity. For her, we are the crossover generation. The time for individual/species transformation to the next phase of evolutionary emergence is now.

That, in a nutshell, is the vision. And it is a vision that is being acted upon and implemented increasingly by citizen groups in various regions. To her credit, Hubbard is the first to admit that the ten-step Emergence Process outlined here is *a* way, not *the* way (for everyone). But it is the way for her and it is a way that has proven effective for those in the core group of the Santa Barbara Conscious Evolution community who agreed to be beta test subjects in the first public use of the approach described here. On their behalf, and for those who will be following this path as well, thank you, Barbara, for the vibrancy of your vision, and the generosity of your heart!

—Oliver W. Markley, professor emeritus of
human sciences and studies of the future
University of Houston-Clear Lake

REFERENCES

Campbell, Joseph. 1968. *The Hero With a Thousand Faces*. Princeton, N.J.: Princeton University Press.

Bucke, Richard Maurice. 1974. *Cosmic Consciousness: A Study in the Evolution of the Human Mind*. New York: Causeway Books.

Teilhard deChardin, Pierre. 1975. *The Phenomenon of Man*. New York: HarperCollins.

Chopra, Deepak. 2000. *How to Know God: The Soul's Journey Into the Mystery of the Mysteries*. New York: Crown Publishing.

Hubbard, Barbara Marx. 1998. *Conscious Evolution: Awakening the Power of Our Social Potential*. Novato, Calif.: New World Library.

————. 1993. *The Revelation: Our Crisis Is a Birth*. Sonoma, Calif.: Foundation for Conscious Evolution.

Campbell, Joseph et al. 1982. *Changing Images of Man*, ed. Joseph Campbell and Willis W. Harman. Oxford, N. Y.: Pergamon Press.

Introduction

Well, here it is.

This is the book you've been waiting for.

This is the book that provides an answer to the question, "How do I get from where I am to where I want to be?"

This is the book that finally addresses the question, "And how does *the world?*"

In startlingly clear and strikingly simple terms, this book lays out a road map to not only a better tomorrow, but a better Here and Now. That makes it both conceptually stimulating and imminently practical. In other words, it's the kind of book you can get excited about, and it's the kind of book you can *use*.

Here you will find a wonderful guide to experiencing your Highest Self. A step-by-step instruction. A flashlight at dusk, a candle in the dark. And you did not come to this book by accident. It is all part of a process of your own emergence, and of the emergence of the entire human race.

To its immense credit, this book does not claim to be *the* way, but simply to be *a* way. That's important, otherwise it could turn into dogma—which is the last thing that its author would want.

Now let's talk about that author for just a moment.

I have known Barbara Marx Hubbard for a number of years. I have known of her for a great many more. That is because Barbara's life and work have touched the world in such enriching ways.

A philosopher and futurist of the first rank, she has written, lectured, facilitated workshops and retreats, acted as a quiet consultant to political, business, and spiritual leaders, and placed the wealth of her mind at the disposal of the human race in countless other ways, large and small, adding much to the treasure that is The Human Experience, and considerably enhancing it.

Anyone who has read one of her books knows what I mean. Anyone who has heard her lecture understands my comments perfectly. Anyone who has been deeply touched and changed forever at one of her workshops nods now in gigantic assent.

And anyone who has asked for her help in thinking through the problems of our times, assessing the challenges and the possibilities of our tomorrows, or charting a course for our future, knows why Barbara Marx Hubbard is regarded across the United States and around the world as a breathtaking visionary and a brilliant conceptualizer whose insights astonish and excite the human heart, and so, are sought after everywhere.

The latest of these insights, and, I believe, the most profound, are now ours to explore in this book. And the benefits of that could be enormous. For what is presented here is not only a new way to understand our human history but a way to magnificently *create* the history of our tomorrows, changing forever our very idea of what it means to be human.

Here is a short but fascinating story of our species and the path it has taken, as well as the path it now has an opportunity to take, as we march together into the twenty-first century. Here is also an emphatically compelling story of individual transformation—a story of Barbara Marx Hubbard's own work with this material, of her own spiritual experiment—that winds up presenting us all with a path to what could well be *our* own grandest human experience.

We can become something that we never were—and have always been. We can create something that we could not have imagined—and that we've always dreamed. We can produce something on this planet that we never thought possible—and that we always knew was probable, sooner or later.

We can do this if we will allow ourselves to explore together, and to take together, the journey to the ultimate realization of our human nature, and the total experience of our divine nature, which are one and the same.

This will take a sincere willingness to deeply understand both the prior limits of our human experience and the unlimited wonder of our human potential—and to turn what we have come to understand into the functioning realities of our daily life.

And it will take opportunity.

That's what you're holding in your hand. If I were called upon to describe this book in one word, I would say: *opportunity.* Because that's what this book represents. And it is an opportunity that you have called to yourself.

So now, read what you were meant to read. Know what you were meant to know. What you have *always* known—and are now ready to act upon.

Your own emergence is at hand.

—Neale Donald Walsch
Author, *Conversations with God*

Part I.
The Emergence Context

The Cross-Over Generation

Something is happening to us.

It is the most important thing that will ever happen to us.

Ours is the first generation—and will be the only generation in human history—to experience it.

You will experience it directly, if you are ready.

What is happening could be called a birth, for in a very real sense, it is the bringing forth of a new being—what I am calling a *Universal Human*. This birth is part of the long developmental process of our species and is in some ways similar to our biological growth. First there is the *Embryonic stage* that marks our earliest development as Universal Humans, and includes the events of our *conception, gestation,* and *birth*. From there, we emerge into a second stage, our *Infancy*. We continue to develop, passing through the next stage of *Childhood*, followed by *Youth*. Finally, we graduate from the early stages and enter *Adulthood*. This final stage, I believe, has not yet been experienced by any of us on planet Earth, because the conditions have not yet called us forth, as we shall soon see.

It is the mysterious process of the Embryonic stage, marked by the events of conception, gestation, and birth, that I believe many of us are in the midst of or have just completed. You will soon know if you are one of those who has experienced this stage.

The completion of my own personal passage through this initial stage has allowed me to move into the experience I call *emergence*. This process begins in our Infancy and unfolds through the subsequent stages of our development. It is my observation that millions of people have, like me, started down the path of their own emergence, the steps of which are described in this book.

In order for you to see where you are in the larger process of your own emergence, I'd like to describe the first, or Embryonic, stage of the Universal Human. But before I do, I want to tell you what we are all emerging *into*, what we are becoming.

A "Universal Human" is one who is connected through the heart to the whole of life, attuned to the deeper intelligence of nature, and called forth irresistibly by spirit to creatively express his or her gifts in the evolution of self and the world. Above all, a Universal Human has shifted identity from the separated egoic self to the deeper self that is a direct expression of Source. To become a Universal Human is to evolve consciously, choosing a path of development that has never been mapped before in a world that has never existed before.

This book charts a course for all of us who are awakening to this new expression of humanity emerging within ourselves, and who are seeking guidance along the way. It is a first spiritual path ever designed *specifically* for this moment in human history; it is a personal path guiding us to participate consciously in the process of creation at the time when conditions on planet Earth are reaching a crisis so deep we may be heading toward a self-induced extinction, or on the other hand, a transformation toward an immeasurable and unknown future. Emergence is a way for those of us who feel called to enter into the co-creation of a new world through the fulfillment of our own life purpose, creativity, and love.

How can you tell if you are one of those who is either in or passing through the early Embryonic stage of your development as a Universal Human?

The first sign you are in this stage is the event of *conception*. This is marked by your being awakened by spiritual experiences, peak moments, and unitive flashes. During the experiences, you have your first tastes of transcending your mind and feel yourself connected to God, to the energy of the whole. You sense that you are more than your personality, your assumed identity. The Essential Self, that deeper yet hidden part of your being that is connected to Source, that is animating and guiding you, is "turned on." If you are fortunate, you have found yourself by circumstance, conditions, and personal openness able to continue nurturing this awareness, and a presence, an Essence, is now growing within you.

At conception, you catch a glimpse of the greater being that you are. You may experience higher guidance and a strong connection to those spiritual ancestors or archetypes who are most in harmony with your metaphysical temperament. You may awaken to a higher destiny through an awareness of what James Hillman calls your "soul's code."

If you are in this stage, you may find yourself catapulted out of your comfort and current life circumstances by a passionate desire to express your creativity—what I call "vocational arousal"—and an urgent wish to find others like yourself. You may experience resonance and communion with other pioneering souls who warm your heart and motivate you to reach out even more. Favorite authors may fall into this category. You may have allowed a lecturer or spiritual leader to touch your life in a significant way.

Having read this, you know already if you have gone through—or are going through—the next event of this stage, that of gestation. For some time, you have been reading books by authors who inspire you, and going to personal development workshops. You are awakening spiritually, getting in touch with higher guidance, inner voices, and expanded experiences.

You have been motivated by a greater calling, and may even be fully engaged in the vocation of your destiny. But you still feel driven, separated, anxious, as if something is missing. This awareness is important. It is a vital sign that you are ready to be born, ready to grow into the next stage of life. Through the whole period of gestation, you are still in the womb of self-consciousness, developing as a Universal Human.

You may be receiving guidance and inspiration from higher sources, but you still feel a sense of separation from the Source of that guidance. The local personality self is still "in charge."

The completion of gestation occurs when you realize you do not, and indeed cannot, continue to grow and develop within the state of egoic, self-centered consciousness.

You hit a definitive limit to growth in your current mode. You may experience confusion, frustration, even depression. Something more is to come. Something more *has* to come.

This is a birth signal, and it marks the end of the Embryonic stage. It is often painful, although it can also be easy and graceful. In either case, you have outgrown the womb of self-consciousness.

I define the event of *birth* as the conscious choice to evolve beyond the identity and control of our egoic, personality selves—what I call the *local self*. It is a time of surrender and openness to something new. It is a transition to an expanded life.

During this transition of *birth*, we are often confused and feel that we are facing the unknown without guidelines or mentors to help us. This feeling is accurate, for we are facing a new condition on Earth. There are no adult Universal Humans who have been through the transition from a high-technology, over-populating, polluting world at the edge of destroying its own life-support systems to a new world that is sustainable, compassionate, and life-enhancing. Still, confused or not, at birth everything we have experienced during our gestation is now bursting to be more fully realized in our lives.

This is what is occurring all over our planet at the present moment. Our personal emergence as young Universal Humans is triggered by a larger *planetary* birth. We are like cells in the body of an infant going through the actual transition from womb to world.

Here's the fascinating reason why:

The Urgency to Evolve

The human family has come to an evolutionary crossroad, and those of us alive today are the cross-over generation, responsible for leading the way from one stage of our species' evolution to the next. The very real salvation of our world depends on this generation developing and embodying in ourselves the qualities of *being* (natural to a Universal Human) that are necessary to make this leap. For in our generation, we have gained unprecedented power on a technological level to destroy this world as we know it, or to co-create a future equal to our full potential.

Each of us is now born into a new and rapidly changing world that demands we evolve in consciousness in order to survive personally, and as a species, much less fulfill our magnificent potential.

What makes our world such a radical departure from that which has preceded it is the enriched and maturing *noosphere*—a term first used by Teilhard de Chardin to describe what we might call "the thinking layer of Earth," or the mind sphere. Think of this noosphere as an invisible, yet all pervasive, superorganism. Here, each of us lives, much as our own cells live inside of our body.

The noosphere is composed of our collective consciousness, our languages, our art, our music, our religions, literature, laws, and ethics, as well as the intelligence that is creating our *extended bodies* in the form of rapidly growing technology: microscopes, telescopes, rockets, faxes, phones, and the Internet.

It is through the genius that is the noosphere that we are able to land on the moon, map all the genes in our bodies—and create bombs that can destroy the world.

Through biotechnology we are already altering the design of life, either creating monstrous life forms or gaining the capacity for conscious birth, chosen death, life extension, understanding aging, cloning, and far more.

Through nanotechnology we may soon be able to build as nature does, atom by atom, learning to regenerate cells, heal disease, travel through space on solar wings as fine as nature itself could create, and possibly even render all polluting technologies obsolete. Or we can misuse this new power and develop self-replicating machines that can destroy our world.

Through space travel we are becoming physically universal, gaining access to untold resources in our solar system and beyond, developing the early capacities of an intergalactic species able to create new, miniature worlds in space. Or, of course, we can build Star Wars instead of Star Worlds, and forever close our chances for expanded universal life.

Through extended media, especially the Internet, we are becoming *one interacting, intercommunicating living system*, in which each human has access to the intelligence of the whole system and can place his or her own intelligence into the whole without gatekeepers. The capacity of computers is increasing so rapidly as to suggest the possibility of a new form of silicon-based life. We can either guide these powers to enhance life, or they can dominate and dehumanize us all.

And it doesn't end there. We are at the threshold of learning how to access zero-point energy to provide limitless energy, now hidden in the plenum of space, for the further growth and development of ourselves not only on Earth but in the universe far beyond our home planet.

These are powers that humans once attributed to the miraculous intervention of gods. But if we are now like gods, then we are not yet wise gods. With these new capacities in our hands we have, *for the first time on Earth*, reached a critical juncture. We must now decide between conscious evolution or extinction through the misuse of our powers.

If enough of us do not transform ourselves into the more universal type of human that I have described (and a path to which I have offered on the pages which follow), our chances of survival as a species are not good.

Our scientists tell us that within as little as one generation—thirty years—our current environmental practices may cause the irreversible degradation or collapse of our life-support systems.

In addition, many of our social systems are dysfunctional, the gap between the rich and poor grows, and billions live in poverty. (Fully half of the world's people are forced to exist on less than two dollars a day—with half a billion living on less than one dollar a day.)

We can read the writing on the wall: The footprint of self-centered humanity is seen everywhere upon the Earth—and the life it is creating is not sustainable.

Our generation has reached Choice Point.

A Crisis of Birth

To understand the meaning of our crises, it is necessary to view them with "evolutionary eyes" that hold the memory of 15 billion years of struggle to evolve, from the first cells gasping for life in the overcrowded seas of the early Earth, to the first humans fighting for survival in an animal world. From this vantage point we can see that, although our current situation is dangerous, painful, and full of suffering, it is also true that the set of breakdowns we are witnessing on all levels—environmental, social, and personal—are actually *evolutionary drivers*, compelling us across our current threshold toward the new Universal Humanity.

The many crises we are undergoing are exactly what are needed to bring about the awakening of our species to the necessity of evolving in our consciousness and capacities. If we respond to these crises with creativity and compassion, our species will have taken a quantum jump. We will be capable of conscious evolution, of co-evolving with nature, of planetary management, of social transformation. A closer look at this breakdown process reveals that, while it is potentially dangerous, it is also natural and ultimately could lead toward the emergence not only of Universal Humans but of a Universal Humanity, a collective cultural, social, and technological global/universal civilization that far transcends our current world.

As an intelligent species with a deep understanding of nature, it is natural and even expected that we would succeed to a point of reaching a limit to growth on our finite planet.

It is natural that we would unknowingly pollute and over-populate, stopping only when we receive feedback signals that our life-support systems are threatened.

It is natural that we would be confused and awkward in our response, learning late in the game that we are responsible for managing a complex ecological system, including waste management and food distribution, on a global scale.

From this larger perspective, we see how we are haltingly shifting from massive procreation to co-creation to the spiritually motivated desire to express our creativity in life purpose and vocation—in many new functions needed for the healing and evolving of our world.

In this process we are discovering something very interesting—and a little shocking to our system. We are finding out that what worked in the past for our survival will destroy us now. It is difficult for some people and some cultures to believe, but it is nevertheless true that the very behaviors that kept us alive in prior times are the behaviors that are threatening to end our lives today.

We are a slowly awakening planetary giant just beginning to realize that we are one living body responsible for its own future in a universe of unknown dimensions.

Human infants experience a similar process of growth shortly after birth. Once in the world, the infant is shocked out of the comfort of the womb, often panicked and screaming, driven by new life conditions to learn to breathe, nurse, eliminate, and coordinate *quickly*. And it is precisely these new conditions that activate the next level of the infant's DNA code, which has in it the blueprint of exactly what to do next but was awaiting the signal of birth.

Now we are back to where I was earlier, when I spoke of what is occurring at present all over our planet. As humans, we are all members of the larger planetary body, living through a period of time analogous to a birth, our planetary birth.

Our crisis is a birth!

Our personal emergence as Universal Humans is occurring at the time of the planetary crisis of birth, when we suddenly have to shift from non-renewable to renewable resources, handle our own wastes, get food to all our members, and coordinate ourselves as a global system. And we must do this quickly, just as a newborn baby must immediately learn to breathe, nurse, and eliminate.

This birth process can be difficult and even deadly, or natural and easy.

New life conditions on our planet require us to shift every function in the living system, causing activation of our own "genius code"—our unique creativity—a design which resides deeper in our body/mind, perhaps even in our yet unused DNA, and in the emergent potential of evolution—in order to produce the capacities and consciousness we need to meet the challenges ahead.

We have always known about this extraordinary activation process. Our ancestors described it by saying, simply, . . . *necessity is the mother of invention.* (Even they used the "mother/birthing" model!)

The "genius code" now being activated is the pattern or imprint for our next developmental stage as we evolve from *Homo sapiens* to *Homo universalis*—the Universal Human.

We can look upon our problems with the gratitude and even awe that a mother feels after laboring in childbirth to bring forth her newborn child. Without this painful passage, these wide-scale breakdowns on all levels of our existence, we might have slumbered forever in self-consciousness.

Crossing the Threshold

In this transition—which is not yet complete, but portions of which we can now look back on—magnificent leaps have already been taken. We have seen ourselves from outer space and discovered that there are materials of many Earths just in our infant-like grasp.

Our environmental movement has arisen, awakening in millions the mystical and pragmatic awareness that we are all members of one living body, connected, response-able, and co-creative with Earth life.

Thousands of organizations have arisen out of love, caring, and commitment to press for social justice, peace, human rights, economic equity, environmental restoration, and far more.

Human and spiritual potential movements abound.

Wherever they have the choice, women are shifting from massive procreation to co-creation. We have reached a limit to population growth on Earth. One more doubling of the population will take us over ten billion. We *will* have fewer children—whether by choice or catastrophe is the only question.

This bio-evolutionary fact is gradually freeing the feminine half of the species from the huge effort to reproduce up to maximum. That creativity is available now for life purpose and expression in the larger world. Out of these breakdowns, innovations and new possibilities are arising to foreshadow not only a new human, but a new world and, indeed, many new worlds in the universe.

Like every birth, the outcome is unpredictable. Yet in this *planetary* birth, you, as a member of the cross-over generation, are capable of choosing to respond as your own evolutionary midwife and deliver yourself as a Universal Human—our next stage of evolution.

We are all capable of doing that. Still, we face the crisis created by this birthing process. That crisis is natural but dangerous. I believe that we will discover *encoded in our collective intuitive and scientific knowing,* hidden in our noosphere, *the genius code—the design of our own conscious evolution* that is required to respond to this crisis, and to actualize the next stage of human development—the Universal Human.

The key is to access this latent design in time. Then we can emerge from the womb of our self-conscious, separated stage to our whole-centered co-creative phase of human existence.

There are ways to achieve this access—and one of those ways is what emergence is all about. As I said, it is designed specifically for this utterly new planetary situation to help usher in and encourage a kind of human who can use our rapidly growing technological and social powers for the enhancement and evolution of Earth life.

I feel sure that those of us who are ready and willing can choose to make this final step in our current transition, and if you have read this far, you have already decided that this includes you; you have self-identified. You can now choose to leap, with others, across a vast threshold on a personal, social, and planetary scale and to use our new powers more wisely to create a future more magnificent than we can even imagine. For, with the very powers that could destroy us, we could become not only Universal Humans, but a Universal Human*ity*—a vastly powerful and loving global/universal culture.

In such a culture, we could restore the Earth, free ourselves from hunger, transform our social systems, liberate our creativity, and evolve far beyond our current biological life cycle to become a species ready to participate in what Eric Chaisson, in *The Life Era: Cosmic Selection and Conscious Evolution* (1987), calls "species immortality, cosmic consciousness, and universal life."

The Invitation and the Challenge

I would like to extend an invitation to all who have worked so hard and labored so long to more deeply understand life and more profoundly enrich it. This is an invitation to join the millions of us so-called ordinary people from every faith, background, and tradition—as well as those who have no religious tradition at all—in awakening to lives that are more holistic, empathetic, spiritually attuned, creative, responsible, and spirit-centered than they ever were before.

Your evolutionary code has been activated or, as just noticed, you would probably not be here, reading material such as this. You and I, and others like us, are emerging into the next stage of human consciousness, not through the vehicle of a new religion but as the *individual fulfillment of what all religions have promised*.

You are taking a New Journey, the journey of the Emergence Process. We are taking it together. And it is quite different from the Old Developmental Path of our collective past.

The new journey of emergence unfolds in a world infused with a vastly expanded noosphere, a world that has truly never existed before. Yet, as we take our first steps on this momentous new journey, we stand on the shoulders of all those who came before us to clear the way. The new path may be untraveled and unique, but the Universal Human has been prefigured in the great avatars, mystics, saints, and scientists of the past.

These advanced humans broke through the limits of self-consciousness into a cosmic, universal level of awareness. Many of them—Jesus, Buddha, Krishna, Mohammed, and others—were great teachers and founded the major religions of the world. They experienced God, the Void, the true nature of reality, the Source of creation directly. Within their cultures, they became examples of humans emerging beyond self-centered consciousness and offered teachings for each individual to follow in order to become that themselves.

In every tradition, these teachings included the concepts of loving one another and doing unto others as we would have it done unto ourselves, as well as the central revelation that we are more than separated physical beings dying in the night.

Ken Wilber sees these avatars as ourselves in the future. He writes in *A Brief History of Everything* (1996):

> And these higher states of human evolution, which in the past have been achieved by the few—the rare, the elite, the gifted, the ahead-of-their time—might actually give us some hints about what collective evolution has in store for us. Evolution is a wildly self-transcending process; it has the utterly amazing capacity to go beyond what went before. I think the sages are the growing tip of the secret impulse of evolution . . . the leading edge of the self-transcending drive that always goes beyond what went before. I think they embody the very drive of the Kosmos toward greater depth and expanding consciousness—they are riding the edge of a light beam racing toward a rendezvous with God.

However, in the past, few among us could actually "ride the light beam" and experience in our own lives what those early Great Ones did. Strongly individualistic nervous systems kept us in a state of apparent separation from one another. We lived short life spans, reproducing up to maximum in scarcity and adversity.

It became the work of religions, with their priests and dogmas, to preserve the teachings of those rare individuals and to prepare us for our own evolution. But because people who followed the great teachers rarely experienced unitive, cosmic consciousness themselves, the formal religions often displayed the very qualities of violence and separation they were designed to overcome.

Now, at this unique point in human history, you come along, with millions of others, able and ready to awaken into a state of consciousness that was formerly achievable only by those rare and elite ones who were ahead of their time. This is not because we are wiser than those who came before, but because we were born at a time of evolutionary change on planet Earth that is calling forth our dormant potential en masse for the first time in human history.

By necessity, our New Journey must begin, and a new path must be created, taking all of those who choose to evolve to a place where the earlier path took only a few.

A New Journey

What is the process each of us must undergo along the new developmental journey to ensure the quantum leap in human evolution so urgently needed on our planet at this time?

This question is answered in part 2 of this book, the Guide to Emergence: A Handbook for Co-creators of a New World, which lays out an intimate and practical process for all those who wish to make the journey through the next stages of human evolution. This Guide was developed out of my own moment-to-moment experiences, some of which is related as I describe the steps on the journey themselves. As you read through this Guide, you and I will take this journey again, together.

I know that it will be an exciting journey. It will be an inspiring one. And it will lead you to places that you may have never gone before. Yet let me say something very clearly, so that if you do choose to take this Journey, as I hope that you will, you will know exactly where you are going.

The process of emergence involves a *fundamental, definitive shift in identity,* one which marks our emergence from the Embryonic stage of development, including the events of our conception, gestation, and birth.

This is a shift from the egoic, self-conscious, personality self—the local self—to the universal, non-egoic, co-creative or divine self—*the Essential Self.* Using our previous analogy, in the Emergence Process the local self actually gives up its dominion and invites the birth of the Essential Self within us. This shift occurs when the driven, anxious local self chooses to stop, to release control, and to invite the higher power, the Essential Self, to come in the whole way. This choice is the great decision that sets in motion the next stage of our evolution.

In my own life, my daughter Suzanne Hubbard inspired and energized me, as she discovered a "Blueprint" for our emergence as Universal Humans. She wrote in her forthcoming work, *The Life Book* (See page 183):

> When we are born as a physical child, we are endowed with . . . two qualities of being. We are the local self who is the biological, egoic, personality self, and we are the Essential Self who is non-local and resonant with the larger reality, the mind of God. In general, we are unconscious of the Essential Self [until our conception,

gestation, and birth]. The evolutionary journey of a Universal Human begins the process that awakens us to our inner being as our Essential Self.

The change in identity we must undergo is marked by the shift from the creature human, who lives life as a self-conscious, survival-oriented person, to the co-creative human, who is inspired by spirit to express and embody divine intent. It is the shift of identity from the guided to the Guide, from the one who seeks to That Which Is Sought. We find that when we question, it is The Beloved within us who responds. And when that shift has occurred, each of us will be able to say without embarrassment, inflation, or egotism:

I am no longer separated from the source of creation.
I am one with the essence that pervades the whole universe.
I am an expression of the process of creation of God.
I am the Beloved I have sought since time immemorial.
I am the presence and process of the divine within me.
I am the voice I hear. I am the guide I follow. I am a co-creator of new worlds.
I think, write, and act as that presence in the world.
I am a young Universal Human. I may forget momentarily who I really am, but I will never go back the whole way. As a baby can never return to the womb, I can never go back to my separated state. I am humble. I have universes to understand, infinite things to learn, but I am born.

Even as our spiritual teachers of the past have paved the way for us, their wisdom and examples offering portals through which we new humans arrive in all our diversity and uniqueness, so, too, the recent movements of expanded consciousness, human potential, spiritual growth, women's liberation, and other progressive social changes have further prepared us for what is to come.

Still, no one can fully chart this New Journey, because the Universal Human we are becoming has not yet fully emerged. To map out a path at this point would be like one of our ancestors developing a psychology for *Homo sapiens* while sitting in a cave 50,000 years ago!

We can begin, however, to look at the first small steps that we must take. And that is what *Emergence* seeks to do in the Guide which makes up the largest part of this text.

Our cross-over generation is not leading toward a more fully matured *Homo sapiens*, or even a God-realized human, but rather toward a conscious co-creator on a universal scale, a being not yet evolved on planet Earth. What is new about this is so original as to be scarcely perceivable.

Stages of the New Journey

We are not going through this birth alone or unaided by a larger process. It is my belief that the challenges, which required heroic spiritual practices in the past (in preparation for our emergence), are easier for our generation because we are part of a larger system, which is itself awakening collectively.

When we look around us we see the threat of environmental collapse and increased poverty and suffering for billions, alongside of large-scale spiritual and social awakening. In part, at least, as I have said, the very breakdowns are driving us toward innovation and transformation. People in every culture and in every land are caught up in the transformation. Indeed, they are *creating* it.

If you saw yourself in my description of the Embryonic stage of this process, you are one of these co-creators. Let's say that you have chosen, or are ready to choose, to make the great choice to release control as a local self and invite the deeper self to come in the whole way. This choice carries us toward the next stages of Infancy, Childhood, and Youth. These stages will be explored in greater detail, with specific guidance, in Part 2: Guide to Emergence: A Handbook for Co-creators of a New World.

Infancy

Once we have made the choice to shift from living out of our ego to living as our Essence, miracles begin to happen. Changes occur. We enter our Infancy as Universal Humans. We are born from our self-conscious stage into something new. During Infancy, we fall in love with that essential, higher self that first awoke in us at our conception, and has been guiding us through our gestation and birth. We train ourselves to focus on it and become magnetized to it, beginning a process of incarnation—full embodiment.

In Infancy, we reach a turning point when we invite the Essential Self to take dominion over all aspects of our local selves, the many sub-personalities making up the inner household of selves. This culminates in the blissful union of the human and divine, the ecstatic fusion of ego and essence. A new vibration begins to course through our bodies, motivating and guiding us toward further self-evolution.

In the past, these experiences were often taken as signals for a person to undertake a religious or spiritual life, moving away from the mundane world. We went to cloistered monasteries or ashrams to work with masters and gurus to focus upon securing this new expanded awareness. Our process was direct and vertical—"inward and upward"—an ascendant path toward self-realization and union with God within, toward oneness with non-dual Reality.

Now, as members of the crossover generation, even in our Infancy, we do not, in general, turn inward and upward toward a religious life, but rather inward, upward, and *outward*, in a more horizontal path to become co-creators in the evolution of our world. By co-creator, we mean someone inspired by spirit, whose genius code is awakened, whose love is expanding as comprehensive compassion for all life, who is reaching out to join with others equally inspired to co-design a world equal to our full potential.

We recognize that we cannot develop personally or aim at individual salvation in a world that is going to hell. The very impulse that in the past turned us toward a mystical life now turns us outward as co-creators. The mystical and the secular fuse.

Childhood

In Childhood, we make the fateful shift of identity from ego to Essence, from creature human to co-creative human. We recognize what mystics have always known and taught—we are expressions of the divine, designing, universal intelligence. We—as our Essential Selves—are the guides that have been guiding us; we are the inner voice. We are the Beloved we have been seeking.

We may be connected beyond ourselves to spiritual beings, higher entities, Christ, God, yet at this phase of our evolution, we also are God becoming person as ourselves. We are incarnating the divine, drawing from all masters and teachers of the past. We move to the phase of active embodiment as universal persons.

In Childhood, we begin to function, on a limited scale and in a protected environment, as an integration of the essential divine self and the local self, that is, a Universal Human. Our former egoic personality, the many aspects of our local self, get educated, empowered, and reintegrated as the eyes and ears, the hands and feet of the Universal Human.

This is the requirement at the time of the planetary birth. We desire to learn how to express our Essential

Selves through our vocations and life purpose. It is, as Jean Houston put it, a "re-genesis," or perhaps a co-genesis.

Youth

Childhood leads very naturally to Youth, when we begin to mature as the Universal Human. The occurrence of this phase in our development is, as yet, quite rare. This is because so few of us have been able to find our life purpose, surrender our egos, create even a small community of kindred souls, and begin our true work in the world. It hasn't been time, but it is now. Many of us are crossing over from Childhood to Youth as we enter the Third Millennium because the world conditions are calling us forth en masse, as I have said.

In Youth, we gain some continuity of consciousness as universal beings, but just as self-consciousness was once unstable in the animal world, so now cosmic or universal consciousness is unstable in the human world. Our goal here is to stabilize unitive consciousness as a new norm. (There is no one agreed-upon word to describe the next stage of consciousness. Use whichever word appeals to you.)

In our Youth, through deep inner work and communion with others doing the same, we stabilize more deeply in our remembrance of our essential nature as an expression of the divine.

In this phase, we begin to "come into form" in the external world, in the co-creation of new projects of all kinds. We are transforming the basic systems of the planetary body now "born" to its next stage of life. We work in all fields—in health, education, business, sciences, the arts and media, government, environment—to recreate a world that is sustainable and capable of manifesting our higher values. We are, as Neale Donald Walsch says in *Conversations with God*, "recreating ourselves anew in the next grandest version of the greatest vision ever we held about Who We Are."

These kinds of activities may still, in most cases, be too small in scale to actually transform the world, but they are harbingers of the new society being built even now by young Universal Humans in every field of endeavor.

In Youth, we shift from the emphasis on sexual reproduction toward "suprasexual co-creation," moving from self-reproduction to self-evolution. Our sexuality evolves and vitalizes all areas of our creativity. We long to join not only our genes to reproduce biologically but our *genius* to give birth to the potential in one another.

We begin to experience the mystery of the fusion of genius and the joy of co-creating. Our progeny become our projects. We often experience optimum health and a feeling of regeneration, even in our later years.

Youth prepares us for the final stage of our development as Universal Humans, Adulthood. My sense is that this stage has never yet been fully experienced in our species, because it hasn't yet been time, organically, in the evolution of our larger planetary body.

I do not believe that the mature stage, the *Adult* Universal Human, will appear until *after* the period of quantum change, when the new phase of evolution has been secured and a critical mass of humans has stabilized at a unitive stage of consciousness. My vision is that, at that time, our Essential Selves will have gained dominion within ourselves en masse, and we will become Universal Humans as a new norm.

This advanced human can appear once we, the pioneering cross-over generation, have successfully passed through this period of transition and have built a sustainable culture which calls forth the Adult Universal Human in all of us. We will then all be born into a vastly enriched social and technological environment, a far more matured noosphere, so radically empowered that it will undoubtedly call forth new potentialities dormant in us during the first "chapter" of our history. (See the Map of the First Two Chapters in the History of the World on page 178.)

Margaret Mead once said that even the most brilliant among us has only used 10% of our full potential. Let's imagine that the untapped 90% potential is awaiting our engagement in the huge challenges of conscious evolution. Let's assume that we are designed to evolve, spiritually, socially, and scientifically/technologically. Let's realize that we are being born into a universe of billions and billions of galaxies.

Earth is a womb for universal life. We have no idea how many other suns are "mothering" baby planets also giving birth to universal life. But this much we can see:

We will probably have access to zero-point energy and find ourselves with abundant, almost infinite, resources.

We will have learned to extend our lives.

We will be living on Earth and in space.

We will have access to the intelligence of the global brain.

We may have made shared contact with other non-human life forms.

The Adult Universal Human is itself a quantum jump. We will have transcended self-consciousness and the "creature human" life cycle. We will then be fulfilling the visions of the future first revealed in mystical revelation, not in life after death but in life after this phase of evolution.

The work of *Emergence* is to assist us as a community and communion of pioneering souls to make the conscious shift now and prepare the way for all generations to come. As we succeed, our descendents will look back with gratitude upon us.

This is the hour when conscious evolution begins. And, as I said at the outset, you can play a decisive role in its activation. You need simply to decide now to take the New Journey; to begin the process of emergence. A guide to take you there—including a description of my own process and ways for you to benefit from it—is a page-turn away.

In this Guide to Emergence, we make this journey together, crossing over in ten concise steps, from our self-conscious, separated, egoic personalities, to God-centered, spiritually motivated, co-creative expressions of the next stage of human evolution. We discover that the higher self that has been informing and motivating us in the early stages of our awakening is not an external force or deity but our own divine self connected to the Larger Whole, or the Godhead.

Through contemplation of this Essential Self, you incarnate it—experiencing it as a tangible, vibrational, *felt* presence—and shift your identity from the egoic personality to the Essential Self. Thus, you begin to cross over from *Homo sapiens* to *Homo universalis*. It is within your power as a member of this cross-over generation to become fully human and fully divine. That is the ultimate goal of the Emergence Process.

Now, before you begin the process . . .

Visualize the evolutionary sequence—*Australopithecus africanus*, *Homo habilis*, *Homo erectus*, *Homo neanderthalensis*, and *Homo sapiens*—as a series of "self" portraits of the long line of emerging humanity. See *Homo sapiens sapiens*, our current representative, developing language, art, religion, ethical systems, democracy, and science, learning at the very last moment, in a "twinkling of the cosmic eye," how nature works, probing the heart of the atom, exploding the first atomic bombs.

Then suddenly, as *Homo sapiens sapiens*, we awaken to the shock of holding in our own hands the powers of co-destruction or co-creation. Feel the flashing awareness of our own possible demise and the dawning recognition that we are responsible for the guidance of these new powers.

Now, in this sequence, place a new figure, a new "self." Still unformed and barely visible, arising from the Ground of the Cosmos, see a new human connected in consciousness to the whole. Feel its ancestors coming forth—the mystics, seers, and visionaries of the human race—passing the torch to this new human.

The time has come for the Universal Human to stand forth upon the Earth.

Part II.
Guide to Emergence:
A Handbook for
Co-creators of
a New World

Guide to Emergence

From a time before Time, the tradition of Story Telling has been used as an effective means of passing on the lessons and the wisdom that humans have wanted to share with each other and with those who they knew would follow. So, too, in this book has that tool been used.

What follows is a guide, and a journey. It unfolds in ten definitive steps to take you through your Infancy, Childhood, and Youth, on your way to becoming a Universal Human. You may use it to take your own journey, and to find out about mine. For I will be describing here a very similar journey on which I have embarked. Offering vital guideposts of emotional material from the spiritual experiences of my life, I have left a trail of clues so that others might make it through this thicket a little more easily, step by step.

I believe that all of us are living, in a very real sense, The Same Story. There may be minor variations on the theme, but the plot is virtually the same. There are the same mysteries to solve. There are the same dangers to encounter. There are the same disappointments and hurts to endure. There are the same joys, the same exhilarations, the same awakenings to experience.

And the same Love to express.

We could treat this all, between the covers of this document, as a purely academic exploration. Or I could have chosen to write a "how to" book. But I think we need to find ways to humanize the insights that all esoteric, philosophical, and spiritual writing can provide if we are to bridge the gap between body, mind, and spirit and produce outcomes that match inputs.

If what we want to see is *application* of important insights in our collectively created daily lives, we must *make them real* for everyone—and the best way I know how to do that is to explain how and why they became real for me.

My Story, then, is an integral part of this Guide. And my hope is that you, when you finish this journey yourself, will pass your own story on to others, that they may also see where they are going by seeing where you went. We do not take this journey for ourselves alone.

As to the Guide itself, I have these suggestions on how to use it:

- First, read through the Guide to understand the entire Emergence Process as described in ten steps. Refer to the Glossary in the Resource Section as needed on page 168. All books referred to in the text are listed in your Conscious Evolution Library on page 173.

- Allow yourself to consider making a profound commitment to your own Emergence Process. If you feel ready, set your intention to go the whole way in this lifetime.

- Set aside a period of time to be in the Inner Sanctuary and experience the full ten steps of the Emergence Process as described in the Guide. You can begin to practice one step a week for ten weeks, or give yourself a spiritual "advance" in which you follow the steps, one after the other, and integrate them into your daily life.

- Begin a Journal for Inner Voice Dialoguing and other exercises, as described in each of the Guide's ten steps.

- If you are so moved, invite two or more kindred souls to do the process with you, sharing each step along the way. (See page 76 for guidance as to how to form an Emergence Circle.)

- In addition we have prepared Emergence Meditations on tape and CD to guide you through every step on the journey. Visit our website (www.peaceroom.org) or write to P.O. Box 4698, Santa Barbara, CA 93140.

Infancy

Step One: Entering the Inner Sanctuary

Infancy! This is the time when the newly born Universal Human emerges from the womb of self-centered consciousness and we begin to realize our new identity as our own higher, Essential Self. We break out of the limits of our egoic identity and, in innocence and humility, make room for something new.

The Story . . .

On my sixty-ninth birthday, I made the choice that started me upon this journey which is now transforming my life. The scene was Marin County, California; it was a cold, rainy January and February 1999. I stayed warm next to my fireplace, while a steady rain came down, giving me a feeling of inwardness and protection. I was alone with a huge project—to write a Conscious Evolution Curriculum for Universal Humans, an educational framework that begins with the Void and covers the origin of the universe through to the present and beyond. (See "Gateway to Our Conscious Evolution," page 155.)

My dining room table was stacked with neatly piled books for every turn on the spiral of the evolutionary path, written by authors whose work had inspired me for thirty-five years. The room was filled with the noosphere, the collective cosmic mind, the evolutionary impulse of humanity.

Yet, in spite of this rich and supportive environment, I found myself to be driven and compulsive about my work, trapped in a struggle to get the job done. Although I was urging and encouraging others to experience a positive future in their lives, now, I was not at peace, and could find no place of rest within. I realized I had to *stop* my life, to make way for something new.

To begin, I decided to arise before dawn and to devote three hours every morning to being silent and alone, long enough to allow something new to happen. In my early morning silence, I created an Inner Sanctuary, a safe inner space where I felt protected, secure, empty, uninterrupted by my own demands or anyone else's. This was a place as profound as the quietest monastery or cave, a place I created within and around myself. I let there be soft music, candlelight, flowers, and above all, peace and quiet.

I set aside time "out of time" to be in the Inner Sanctuary. But even at the thought of doing this, my compulsive, egoic self—local self—was prickling. I was bombarded by its loud complaint: "We don't have time; we'll never get the Curriculum done." My driven local self always felt "behind" no matter what time I woke up and began my work.

But I persisted. Every morning, I simply sat in silence, open and empty, listening to the crackling fire and the rain drumming softly on my roof. I offered my burdens and responsibilities as sacrifices at the threshold of the Inner Sanctuary, literally laying them at the entrance before I entered into my meditation. I imagined myself as a pilgrim in front of a temple, purifying myself before entering. When the compulsive local self prodded me with, "You forgot to call so-and-so!" or "What are you going to have for lunch?" I resisted, no matter how magnetic the pull. I felt like the mythological Odysseus, strapped to the mast of his ship to prevent himself from succumbing to the temptation of the Sirens. My egoic need to be working was my temptation. I let it go by.

Within my Inner Sanctuary, I created a special writing space, a quiet time following my meditation to gain more intimate access to the wise and beloved inner voice, the Essential Self, that had guided me all my life. This was a voice I'd heard many times, sometimes coming to me in intuitive flashes, but more often, when writing in my journal, it flowed as a stream of ideas emerging from a deeper awareness than my conscious mind. Whenever I felt this flow of inspiration, I relaxed, listened, felt joy, and received guidance from my higher self. It was a motivating presence that had been with me since my origins as a young girl living with my family in New York City. I had been raised with no religion, no metaphysics, no idea of any kind of greater existence, and so this inner voice became the agent of transformation in my life.

While I had no idea of this then, I know now that all of us have this inner voice. It is the Higher Self, the Essential Self, within each of us—which *is* each of us—and it is communicating with us all of the time. Sometimes we hear it, and sometimes we don't, but it is never really silent.

My childhood having passed, and my experience with this beloved inner voice having deepened through the years, I'd come to realize that it was a part of my life that I wanted to expand, to experience more of. Then, I made the decision to create my own Inner Sanctuary. And, after my morning meditation, I went to my writing table and allowed the inner voice to write. One morning, shortly after I began this practice, these words flowed from my pen:

> There are no demands on you now but to rest in my arms—the Inner Beloved—who is one with God. Rest in me. Release all cares. Your work is over as a local self. . . . I am now preparing the way for you to enter into the world as who you really are. Rest in peace. Do your yoga and your journal as you rise at dawn each day for the next twenty-one days. *Be still*. This is your time of communion. Do not hesitate now. By remaining *still* for long enough with me during these twenty-one days, the alchemical process will be set at the next stage of your evolution as a Universal Human.
>
> I want you to rest in the arms of all others who are also transcending now. You are not alone. Feel their strength and know that you are part of them, they are part of you, and that your function is to be an expression of them. You are part of all who are transcending. Patterned within all of you is a new humanity. This is the purpose of the Curriculum you are writing. It evokes the emergence of students into their own Universal Humanhood.
>
> Follow precisely the path I dictate to you for the next twenty-one days. That is what it takes. Everything has been prepared for you to take this final step alone. Then you may join other co-creators as an expression of the new human. But you must take this time now to secure the incorruptible connection.
>
> Now is the greatest leap of faith for you. Have utter faith in me. Achieve deep peace. Be prepared for a great force to enter your life to do this work. It cannot enter till you have achieved deep peace. Your reward for peace that can only be achieved by faith is contact with the force and the forces waiting in the wings.

I was thrilled with this guidance. An electric excitement awakened a deep sense of expectancy in me.

The Guidance . . .

Your own inner voice, as you access it through your meditation and writing in the Inner Sanctuary, will offer you guidance, inspirations, and practices as well. That guidance, when added to the guidance in these pages, will create for you a unique manual for the emergence of the Universal Human you are now becoming.

I strongly advocate cultivating an inner receptivity, an inner listening and attunement to the signals of the Essential Self guidance or inspiration as a practice at this time. These intuitions are the way the deeper self informs us and guides us.

Create an Inner Sanctuary

To begin, set aside time to sit quietly every morning for as long as you can with your journal beside you in peaceful contemplation. This may be very familiar if you have meditated before; any practice you are used to will work to quiet the mind and prepare the inner field. The Emergence Process is not a substitute for any basic practices you are already doing but rather an extension or deepening of them.

Set aside a period of time for an at-home spiritual "advance." You can do this simply by arising earlier than usual every morning and using the extra time for this practice. Peter Russell, author of *The Global Brain Awakens*, *Waking Up in Time*, and *From Science to God,* calls his morning hours his "daily Sabbath," a time for God to come through the whole way. Choose a time in your life to begin this "advance" when you will not be distracted or interrupted by any major life crisis or transition, such as a journey, a divorce, a move. Once the Emergence Process is deliberately started, it is preferable not to stop it abruptly. If the early morning hours don't work for you, choose another time. The Dalai Lama meditates at least four hours a day and travels all over the world. We don't have to be in a cloister to begin this process, but some kind of intensification of focus is essential. Remember, you are preparing for a rendezvous with destiny!

Focus Attention on the Inner Guide, the Essential Self

In your silent time, recall as much as you can of the guidance or inspiration you've already been in touch with—the actual feeling tone of your intuitive experience—and also any qualities you remember about this evolutionary impulse that has motivated your process of transformation. You may recall those experiences that occurred during your gestation phase of development. Remember how warm and safe you felt. Feel the intimacy and compare it to the feeling of anxiety and compulsiveness that characterizes the local self.

If you ask for the Essential Self to come into your consciousness, it will signal you in some way or another, not necessarily like mine does, and not necessarily in written words. It may happen in flashes, insights, images, or hunches. Watch for synchronicity to show up in your life, a phenomenon described by Carl Jung in his book *Synchronicity: An Acausal Connecting Principle* (1969) as "the meaningful coincidence of two or more events, where something other than the probability of chance is involved." Intuit the meaning of synchronicities, as James Redfield recommends in the *Celestine Prophecy* (1995). This is critical. Notice everything with a heightened awareness. The signals will come, because it is the very heart's desire of the Essential Self to communicate with you.

When you ask it to communicate more clearly, it will—one way or the other. Expect the unexpected and anticipate the new!

Release the Pressure of Time Running Out

There is nothing you need to do or accomplish in the Inner Sanctuary. See if you can feel "off duty." Every time you feel the pressure of the thought of time running out, release it. Don't fear, you will still be able to be on time. But releasing the pressure provides the vital freedom needed in the Inner Sanctuary for the inner voice, the Essential Self, to flow forth. It is vital that you inform your local self that there is "all the time in the world," or even better, that you reside in eternity. This is what Ram Dass meant when he said, "Be here now."

In the past, I always had good reasons for not taking the time to practice in this way. Looking back, what I was really telling myself was: I don't have time to be born! I know now that it's an affliction of the local self-consciousness to get its priorities backwards, and that there is nothing more important we can do than give top priority to our own process of emergence. There is no greater gift we can give to those we love than ourselves evolved.

Sometimes when I am walking or sitting silently in nature and I want to feel "off duty," I turn on my internal answering machine to pick up the stream of incoming messages from local self—that endless "to-do list" that seems to pop up whenever I attempt to be still within myself. I place on the internal answering machine an outgoing message to assure local self that its requests have been recorded and it can relax, knowing its "urgent" messages will be responded to at a later time. I have trained my memory to go back, after my walk or meditation, and check those incoming messages. In this way I don't forget what local self had requested and can respond as I choose.

Journal

Inner Voice Dialoguing

Keep a journal of inner voice dialogues so you can recognize and establish a relationship with your own Inner Guide.

For me, this was a key practice in preparing me for my own emergence. I have tracked my inner voice since I began keeping a journal at age eighteen and have continued to record the inner messages all my life, accumulating over 140 volumes of personal writings.

.My practice was to write a morning letter to "Dearly Beloved." I would state my current situation as clearly as possible, making friends with current reality. Then I would ask a question beginning with the phrase, "Dearly Beloved, What does this mean?" or "What is your guidance?" Then I developed a quiet mind, with no preconceptions whatsoever, as to what the response would be. Often extraordinary guidance and gentle wisdom would flow forth. I could identify the presence of the inner knowing by my feeling of relaxation, relief, and renewal. I discovered that this inner knowing is always present.

Gradually, as my emergence continued, I realized that there was no reason to refrain from accessing that voice all the time, in my speaking, knowing, and acting, as well as my writing. I found that when I don't access the voice, it wells up and signals me through a sense of depression or confusion. Depression is often a signal of a growth impulse that is attempting to attract your attention. The key is to respond and seek the deeper meaning behind the pain.

For your first journal exercise, write and describe from memory those key experiences you had of inner guidance during your gestation phase. This will help you get acquainted with the Essential Self, by bringing it to your conscious attention. What did the voice or inspired thought tell you? What did it feel like? Describe any experiences you have had of your Essential Self, any messages or guidance that you have received, any qualities you have noted that characterize the inner guide.

Once you have done this, try this exercise: Write a letter addressed to "Dearly Beloved," or whatever name you choose for your Essential Self. Describe your current situation as precisely as you can, the good and the apparently difficult. Ask the most important questions you may have, as clearly as you can; then release all thought, have no preconceptions. Develop the habit of a poised mind, like a sailboat on a calm sea waiting for the wind.

Our purpose here is precise. It is to establish direct contact with the inner voice, the still, small voice of God expressing as your Essential Self. Start writing any sentence as the inner voice, and see what unfolds. Do not edit, judge, or correct anything. If nothing comes, that is fine. Continue to be still.

If you have been hearing an inner voice and writing in your journal before, this process will be relatively easy. If you have not yet tried this, simply follow the steps with no expectations. Whatever happens will be helpful, this much I know for sure. Everyone has within a deeper, wiser, all-knowing self.

Step Two: Contemplating the Glory of the Beloved

With the creation of an Inner Sanctuary, we have established the field of readiness for our emergence as Universal Humans. In the stillness, we may have felt the presence of our Essential Self, or perhaps a sense of expanded awareness and wholeness. At this stage, we are like the biological infant when it begins to sense itself as a separate entity, a "self." In our Infancy as Universal Humans, the self we are becoming aware of is the Essential Self, the higher self. Now, in this next step, we are ready to fully contemplate this Essential Self in its more personal form, the inner "Beloved," and bring our focus to the specific qualities and wisdom of this all-knowing inner presence.

The Story . . .

Although I have heard and been directed by this inner voice of my higher self for most of my life, I had never focused my local self's attention directly on it until undertaking this process. Before, I asked, listened, heard, wrote, and then acted according to what I'd heard. I communed with God and Christ, but all the while feeling the divine, the deity, to be outside and beyond myself—separate.

The inner words I heard passed *through* me to the page on which I wrote, but did not *become* me. I had never contemplated the actual essence and presence of my own higher self, so that I could feel it, consume it, incorporate it into my flesh and bones—*incarnate it*—until now.

As I turned inward toward this presence, I began to experience a sense of homecoming, of peace and safety, yet at the same time, I was filled with excitement and anticipation. I noticed the qualities of this beloved self who had been signaling me from afar for so long.

She—for the presence, to me, was distinctly feminine, as is this embodiment I am—was not merely an abstracted, "floating" inner voice. Nor was this voice identifiable as the usual impersonal God of the cosmos, or even as the more personal Saint Michael, St. Germaine, or Jesus Christ. Whereas before, I had experienced this presence as Christ or God, now, as I placed my attention on the presence day by day, she seemed to become more real, almost tangible to me. She seemed to be myself! Yet my sense was of a magnificent presence, far beyond my current personality or gender. What I now experienced was a full range of attractive and familiar qualities of the Beloved that had been flickering at the edges of my consciousness all these years.

At first, the presence I felt was a huge shimmering field of light, but as I contemplated deeply, more personal qualities entered my awareness. She is a visionary, a seer. Yet she is warm, motherly, cozy, tender, like the mother I lost when I was twelve. She loves me unconditionally. She knows everything I ever ask her.

The Essential Self, the beloved presence that I am, the source of the early unitive flashes I experienced during my gestation phase, was becoming familiar. I realized that I know this Essential Self better than I know my anxious local self. I am in love with this self, in contrast to my irritated, pressured, and compulsive ego. Yet this self, which I now recognized as omnipresent in my consciousness, did not become revealed until I, from the viewpoint of my local self, put attention on it in the Inner Sanctuary.

The experience in the Inner Sanctuary began to pervade my day with its current of joy. As I went about my work, I felt as though an alchemical process had begun to turn on within me. Warm currents of electricity, very pleasant and calming, flooded my physical experience. Ripples of joy swept gently through me. I noticed that a light euphoria had replaced my chronic anxiety.

My nervous system stopped being irritated by compulsive thoughts. The constant feeling of being rushed slowly but surely faded. If I awoke with the old twang of anxiety, I recalled my experience of the Beloved, and the nervousness seemed to disappear.

To my delight, I noticed that this process *in itself* was self-rewarding. Like the proverbial carrot on the end of a stick, the peace and pleasure I was now experiencing in my daily life motivated me to spend more time in the

Inner Sanctuary to contemplate, feel, and enjoy the glory of the Beloved.

Several days into the process, I wrote in my journal, beginning in the voice of my local self and addressing the Beloved as I had always done:

> Dearly Beloved,
>
> I have come home to you now. I have created the Inner Sanctuary in my little apartment and am here now with my communion and meditation—the fire, the music, the flowers, the flickering candle light, the symbol on a piece of the dollar bill I have placed in a frame (the pyramid with the cosmic eye, and the phrase Novus Ordo Seclorum—new order of the ages). You have infused me with your joy at last. I felt this morning, when I awoke, that instant nervous anxiety, but the connection with you was there, strong enough to withstand the fluctuations of the nervous system. I felt my nervousness batter against the connection like waves against a mighty wall. The wall stood. The protection was there. The door was closed. I feel deep in my solar plexus that something is healing, is knitting together.

I had been feeling a deep sense of anxiety that I could not bring my mission to fulfillment, that "I" would fail. Of course, I realize that this fearful, anxious "I" was my local self, yet my local self is the one who has been carrying the burden of searching and executing. It was my local self who received signals and guidance and tried to act upon them. Now the local self was being absorbed into the Essential Self and began to relax and release its anxiety.

I ask now, Beloved, what is your word for me today? The answer came:

Every morning, as you write in this intimate way, you will be tapping into the glory that is being revealed in you, all of you. Do not think at all about your morning. We have a surprise for you that will bring joy into your heart and light into your eyes.

What is this surprise?

The surprise, dearly beloved, is you now writing directly as a Universal Human to the Universal Human in others. It is your coming out of the closet as yourself in such a way that others will be encouraged to do the same. Above all: Don't think about this.

It is thinking that is your "problem." Each morning after your communion with me, I want you to write without thinking until the Universal Human that you are is writing directly to the Universal Human in millions of women and men. Give it no thought. Let it unfold. Write as long as the pen will flow. You are uncorking a Big Bottle here! This is what we promised you. This is the reward of union with Me. It is union with yourself. It is the life and the light and the love that you are, that each of you is, speaking direct, now.

This kind of writing is the next step after so-called "channeling." It is expressing directly as the Great Creating Process Itself, personally. It is the process of the incarnation of deity. It is God expressing as you, each of you.

You are not to leave the Inner Sanctuary—ever. You are to carry it with you wherever you are. In this Sanctuary you emerge fully as a Universal Human.

It is important that you come to feel your own presence at all times. The disconnect comes when you lose the feeling connection with who you really are.

Can you feel Me now?

Yes, I can. I feel a sort of gentle excitement and anticipation.

> Yes, that excitement is Me, the One who is you, who loves you, who guides you. It is this one who is writing. She is now coming through the door. Feel the door dissolve. Feel Me go through it like neutrinos through walls. Feel Me dissolve the barrier between you and Me until we become as One. Let Me float forward in your consciousness until I am in dominion over your whole body-mind. Let Me through, Barbara, beloved. Let yourself dissolve into Me. Let your self-centered mind be completely absorbed into Me. Let Me heal and regenerate your macular degeneration [age-related loss of vision] so that you can see clearly again. I told you that you were losing your sight because you had narrowed your vision to become useful in the world. This *was* useful, beloved, but it is no longer useful. What is needed now is your *full blown, full frontal presence* emerging as who you truly are.

The Guidance . . .

The next step in the Emergence Process is very simple, yet profound. Often, as I have mentioned, we have recognized the divine outside ourselves. We have prayed to the higher power, we have worshipped God in many forms, or we have identified ourselves with the Infinite, non-dual Reality, losing all sense of a personal self.

Occasionally, mystics experienced the divine within, but as mentioned above, very few of us could hold this state of consciousness. Instead, we relied on priests, master teachers, or divine beings who seemed far beyond our intimate knowing. Now, due to the phase change on planet Earth, when humans are gaining the power to co-destroy and co-create, our relationship with the divine is changing. We are no longer children; we must become conscious participants in the process of creation. And, in fact, countless people are becoming ever more connected to the larger whole, both internally through spiritual attunement and electronically through information media.

I believe that as Universal Humans we will gradually learn to incarnate deity, or the divine, realizing that each one of us actually is an expression of the process of creation. We are *that* in unique form. We are not, and never have been, separate from the Source of our being. It was an illusion caused by self-consciousness in the early phase of *Homo sapiens* before the emergence of the Universal Human. As we cross over from ego to essence, we recognize that we always have been one with the Great Creating Process itself, or God.

The Emergence Process is based on the experience that the Essential Self in each of us is "ripe and ready" to come in the whole way—if we make the conscious choice to focus our intention upon that deep self within. Now is the time of our emergence.

So, during the time you have set aside for being in the Inner Sanctuary, consciously turn the sunlight of your attention inward to focus upon that deeper self in whatever way you experience it: the God-within, the Beloved, the inner voice or guide, the intuitive wisdom that has been, one way or the other, guiding you all along. We are calling it the Essential Self. Use any name that is familiar to you.

Turn the attention of your local self away from its worldly considerations toward this inner presence that is connected to non-dual Reality. This takes focus and high intention. Every time the local self tries to escape into separation—into some distracting thought of what needs to be done, turn it back to the Essential Self. You will find that you know this Essential Self, love this self, and in fact are magnetized by this self. It is your Essential Self! But it has been awaiting the attention of the local, egoic self's conscious regard. You will recognize it because it is profoundly familiar, even if you have never been aware of it before.

Essential Self-Contemplation

The key practice, once the Essential Self emerges in consciousness, is Essential Self-contemplation. To do this, spend as much time as possible allowing the magnetic needle of your attention to drift inward and upward to focus on the felt presence of your inner self. Contemplate the specific qualities of essence that you most love. Self-affirm that these qualities are you.

By this attention, you will materialize the very highest qualities that you seek in yourself. These are all the qualities that the ego has been seeking by its efforts in the world. Joy. Peace. Security. Love. Wholeness. Wisdom. All these qualities are continuously present in the Presence. The more you focus on them, the more they penetrate your being. Your attention manifests them in your awareness and incarnates them as you.

Do this, not only in the Inner Sanctuary but also during the day. Expand your consciousness to include awareness of your Essential Self in everything you do. When you are walking down the street, notice the presence, feel the warmth, attune to the inner voice. Gradually, we learn to keep the practice alive all day, always.

Become the Director of Your Attention

See if you can train your attention to seek a new resting point, a new base state. Instead of letting it flicker and then alight on current problems or situations, gently guide it inwards and upwards toward the beloved presence within. You'll know that you have succeeded when a feeling of warmth and pleasure infuses your nervous system.

Staying with this practice creates a new "strange attractor," a magnetic field within you, as you learn to be sensitive to this excellent biofeedback signal. The moment you feel the pang of ego expressing through anxiety, irritation, anger—stop. Breathe. Return to essence. We are training the inner muscle of attention to be spontaneously attracted to essence as a new norm. For spiritual athletes, this is a vital and ongoing practice.

Forget Your Local Self

Don't be forced by the local self to pay attention to some pain, problem, or circumstance. We know that whatever gets our attention gets us, and so it follows that whatever quality of being we focus on grows within us. As the local self is occupied contemplating the glory of the Beloved—the radiant presence of the Essential Self—it stops focusing on its problems. It loses its grip on your psyche and begins to become self-forgetful. This is very good news!

The longer you can keep your attention on the Beloved, the more steady and ongoing will be the alchemical process that this focus brings. The emotions of warmth and joy are signals that the process is continuing.

We now know that emotions have an underlying biochemical process, fully coordinated by the body/mind on a physiological level. Dr. Candace Pert has documented this and reports in her book, *Molecules of Emotion* (1997), that emotions are communicated directly from cell to cell via tiny biochemical signals. We have also learned that grief or anger or any prolonged negative emotion can cause hours of downtime for the immune system, directly affecting the health of the body.

The Design Is Perfect-Making

Whatever happens may not be what we would have consciously chosen. Often it is not. But when we examine it in the Inner Sanctuary, we find that at the deeper level the situation is not perfect but it "perfects" us to face it, if we choose to accept the challenge. We may experience trauma, tragedy, obstacles, but they can be interpreted as opportunities for growth, designed for our own perfect-making.

The Inner Beloved can be called upon to offer the wisest possible response to the crisis, whatever it is. At this stage, everything is meaningful. Apparently difficult experiences can be reinterpreted as precise openings for self-evolution. Facing the conditions of life exercises and strengthens the Beloved, calling forth the deeper joy of our essence underneath the struggle and pain.

Since I have committed to "go the whole way" in this lifetime, I choose to interpret everything that happens to me as an opportunity for self-evolution. I tell myself that if I did not need to learn from a particular experience I would not be given it. With this understanding, I prefer to face a painful experience now rather than later, because if I face it fully now, I will learn the lesson and not have to deal with it at some future point.

Discipline of Relaxation

The sign of the local self dominance is tension. The local self feeds on stress. Whenever you notice that familiar twang of the nervous system, it is a biochemical signal that local self has taken over, and that you are separated in consciousness from your essence. This is the fundamental cause of the chronic anxiety that afflicts most of us in the modern, secular world.

The minute you feel the tension, stop, breathe, smile, and refocus on the Beloved. You are gaining two skills. The first is you are becoming director of your attention. The second is you are consciously fostering the alchemical process that is now beginning to work toward your transformation. You are in charge of your attention, which is vital to your emergence.

Journal

Describe Your Essential Self

In your journal, describe any experiences you have had of your Essential Self, any messages or guidance that you have received, any qualities you have noted that characterize the Inner Guide, the voice of the Beloved, the evolutionary impulse that has motivated you to transform. Use whatever language works best for you. We do not want to be divided by semantics. There are no fully agreed-upon words to describe these experiences. I tend to use evolutionary words to bridge the gap between the spiritual and the scientific worlds. Each of us can make a contribution to the languaging of our experiences so as not to divide but to include.

Step Three: Incarnating

Our Infancy is maturing. Just as a newborn baby begins to live in the awareness that it is no longer in the womb but born into a new sense of self, we emerging Universal Humans leave behind our former self-consciousness and become aware of our Essential Self much of the time. An infant experiences comfort and peace when held in the arms of its mother. Its panic is calmed as it learns to breathe, nurse, eliminate, and coordinate its newborn self. It begins to smile and feel at home in the "new world" beyond the womb.

So, as we mature as infant Universal Humans, we gain a sense of assurance in our new identity beyond the womb of self-consciousness. The Essential Self begins to come in the whole way. We gain a feeling of peace and joy as the local selves relax their fears and let go of their efforts to control.

The Story . . .

As I spent time in the Inner Sanctuary, contemplating the exquisite qualities of the Essential Self, and as I allowed problems either to pass through, or was willing to consider them as gifts and seek their meaning, the Beloved began to come in further, to substantiate within myself, to incarnate.

In this process, I could physically feel this deeper self as a vibrational field penetrating through my heart and down into my solar plexus, where the knot of anxiety of local self's concerns seemed to dwell like a cold and resistant tumor of trouble, regardless of external situations. Beloved warmed the "cockles of my heart," as they say, and even began to melt the cold, hard knot of clenched emotions in the solar plexus.

I noticed that, as the Essential Self came in further through the attention of the local self, various aspects of the local self relaxed their grip upon the conscious mind. In fact, much to my delight, I found that my compulsive local self was lifted up into the vibrational field of the Beloved. I thought of the words of Jesus: "If I be lifted up, all will be lifted up unto me." In this case, the "I" that is being lifted up is the divine essence, lifted up by focused attention. The "all" are the many aspects of the local self which are intent upon essence. Their illusion of separation is dissolving.

In the process of incarnating, we discover that the sense of separation which the ego so often feels is actually *not* real. According to the modern-day avatar Adi Da (also know as FreeJohn Da), the ego is not an entity but rather a "self-contraction."

He describes his own process in *The Dawn Horse Testament*:

> A profound submission of attention and the total energy of the body-mind to observe, feel, and feel beyond the self-contraction [the anxieties of the local self] and the second, which is coincidental with the first, and ultimately superseded it, was communion with the condition that is simply and directly obvious when the self-contraction is transcended or no longer is effective as a mechanism of dissociation from what is already always the case. . . . It is unnecessary to presume or suffer or be motivated by the self-contraction. In any moment of my direct observation of it . . . a spontaneous release occurred . . . what is always and already is revealed when the self-contraction is not effective. It is revealed to be Self-Radiant Transcendental Being, God, Truth or Happiness. . . . The way is to realize and be the transcendental, unconditional divine self.

The fundamental human problem out of which all others spring is, I believe, the illusion that we are separate from each other, from nature, and from Spirit. As we continue to place our attention on the Essential Self, the illusion fades. We remember our deeper identity most of the time. This identity, of course, is not a personal ego but a personal essence, a unique expression of unconditional reality, or God.

In the Inner Sanctuary, it felt as if the patterns of my local self—the compulsive thoughts—were being erased quickly by the vibrational field of the Beloved. The local self couldn't quite remember what it wanted, for in fact, it didn't really want anything anymore! Why would it, when it was beginning to enjoy the unconditional love, which is the inner ambiance of the Beloved?

The experience was like coming into the warmth after having been out in the cold. There by myself, on the rainy mornings in my little condo in Marin, I was experiencing a natural "high." Only instead of taking a substance to induce a high, I was becoming the new substance myself! This natural, sustainable high, I realized, was becoming available as a new norm.

I felt as though I was falling in love with my Essential Self, an inner love affair. A deep and genuine experience of happiness, independent of my work, infused me, and this startled me. The "starter button" of compulsive thoughts— *Do this! Do that!*—commanding me at six in the morning and before I went to bed at night, stopped stressing my nervous system. The workaholic aspect of my local self subsided. For the first time in a long time, I felt at peace.

I had not been this happy since I was a child, before my mother's death when I was twelve. Over the years, I had scarcely realized this, always placing my attention on my life's purpose rather than upon the evolution of my self. True, my vocational purpose was my pleasure, but, as I said, my work had been taken over by attachment and compulsion. Now, at last, there was a shift of focus from *doing* to *being*, a shift which eventually frees vocation from the egoic attachment, allowing it to come forth unimpeded by anxiety and self-criticism, as a flow of creativity.

Now, as the inner process took hold, the outer work began to take shape effortlessly. Plans that I had been working on for years began to manifest easily as I spent time in the Inner Sanctuary. The work on the Conscious Evolution Curriculum flowed. I was literally organizing every major concept I had ever had in thirty-five years, complete with books, references, and quotes from key thinkers illuminating the evolutionary story from the Void through the Big Bang and into the present and beyond. Professors and academics became interested. People were excited and awaited each module.

My partnership with my daughter Suzanne deepened as she intuited her "Blueprint" of personal conscious evolution which seemed true to both of us. I was no longer feeling cut off but in fact was becoming connected at a deeper level than I'd ever experienced before. (This experience foreshadowed the complete repatterning of my life that occurred later in the process, demonstrating how inner integration leads to outer manifestation of our deepest values and aspirations.)

I continued the journal writing and began to describe the situation in my morning letter to "Dearly Beloved."

> The purpose of this writing is to bring myself through. I am not to write anything for others until I AM THAT as a steady presence that I can sense, touch, feel, and be. I am to become substantial as myself. This is known as bringing yourself "through the veil."
>
> I now understand what is happening to me. There was in me such an overriding compulsion to "fulfill my mission" that I continually put the purpose of being myself second, not first. Now, by grace, in the month of February 1999, I have finally taken the time and space to both bring myself through the veil and to write the Conscious Evolution Curriculum.

Even as I wrote, I felt a flash of the old anxiety pulling at me. There was a little tug at the center of my solar plexus that seemed to say, "Get to work . . . it's 8:30 A.M.!"

The inner guide responded:

> When the pull of anxiety comes, let it be. Be still. Put this purpose first. Do not act upon the temptation to "get things done" at the expense of nourishing, flourishing, nurturing the Presence that I AM. When you feel the anxiety, just let it be.

> This is the initiation. On the subtle planes, it is the process of transubstantiating yourself through communion with the divine within yourself as well as beyond yourself.

I had never "Put This Purpose First." The desire to fulfill my mission, given me by the inner voice, compelled me to action, in such a way that I did not fully remain connected to the Source of the guidance. That has been the crux of the disconnection which must be healed for this initiation to complete itself.

I wrote:

> I humbly surrender the temptation to manifest in the world for the reality of being the manifestation I am seeking and unfolding the expression from that vantage point. This is my calling now.

I was seeing how my personal experience related to the bigger picture of conscious evolution and to the quantum shift we are undergoing as a species. Since our world is evolving, so obviously are we, as I have said before. Experienced to its fullest, this Emergence Process may well engender an actual alchemical transformation on a planetary scale. When we learn to stay in this state over time, we will live in a continuous, sustainable resonant field of co-creation, creating a new culture for a new humanity—a Universal Humanity—that reflects our higher state of being.

I believe that this process will actually transform the density of our bodies to bodies that are lighter and more sensitive to thought and intention. We will find that we are potentially capable of feats now considered meta-normal or paranormal, as demonstrated by so many of the yogic traditions. Our emergence is the signal that activates these dormant capacities, calling them forth for a new humanity.

The Guidance . . .

In the Inner Sanctuary, we continue to place our attention on our Essential Self, which we experience as a vibrational energy field, the radiant presence of the Beloved within. This presence enters our inner awareness, releasing stress and anxiety, filling us with a gentle joy, lightheartedness, confidence, and a growing trust in the process beyond the confines of our rational minds. When an addictive thought pattern arises in the Inner Sanctuary, such as "I am a failure," it is quickly erased in the vibrational field of the Beloved already established.

Now we enter a new phase in our development. When the local self, by its own intention, repeatedly places its attention on the essence of its being, we begin to vibrate at a higher frequency. The Essential Self seems to change our very physical substance from density to lightness, from contraction to free-flowing energy. We experience our essence as substantial. It feels as though the Essential Self is incarnating, entering our body/mind and transforming it as our local self resonates to the higher frequencies of the Essential Self. We are entering the next stage of the continuing incarnation of the divine in human form.

A. H. Almaas, in his seminal work *Essence* (1986), tells us that essence is "not only a concept, an image, an archetype, or a state of mind. Rather, it has precise and definite physical characteristics." Essential self-transformation is, in other words, really a tran*substantiation*—a change in the substance of our being.

Put This Purpose First

The key practice at this stage is to continue putting the purpose of being essence first, not second. This does not mean we stop doing everything else in our life. It simply means that whatever we are doing, we keep our primary focus of attention on the Beloved within. In the Inner Sanctuary, continue Essential Self contemplation and practice radiating the warmth and presence of the Beloved within yourself. Do this especially if a local self acts up and you feel anxiety, or lack of self esteem, or rejection. Radiate the presence directly upon the wounded self, like a mother's embrace to a frightened child, comforting and calming.

All day, every day, as you leave your meditation, make of your life a continuous process of placing your attention on the presence of the Essential Self. The local selves will begin to experience a deep attraction, a desire to remain in the presence of this beneficent being, rather than to stray outward in anxious efforts. The magnet of your attention begins to draw to it wayward thoughts. They will continue to occur, but you will find that as long as you keep your attention on the source of your inspiration, the local self will release its grip on you. You will begin to feel a new freedom from anxiety, pressure, and compulsions.

Close the Door

As was described in the previous step, local self has a way of escaping out the back door of the Inner Sanctuary. Just as I am contemplating essence, local self will send in a thought—"We must get busy writing the Curriculum!"— which begins to pull my attention away from my focus on essence. That prickly feeling of irritation clouds the Inner Sanctuary. Before I know it, I am interrupting my time in the Inner Sanctuary, dialing a phone call to some professor!

For me, it became necessary to declare, without equivocation, that there was absolutely nothing local self could do, on its own, that would bring peace or real satisfaction. No matter what the temptation—one more book, event, or success—it will not lead to fulfillment of myself or the work, if done for the purpose of trying to fill up the emptiness inside. Whenever the local self attempts to get out the door to satisfy itself through manipulation of the external world, it finds it irrevocably closed. No escape! This sounds overly absolute, perhaps, but I found it worked.

Journal

Describe Your Essence

Before sitting down to write, take time to feel your essence. Love it. Allow it to substantiate further and further. It will come into your attention if you focus on it. Describe what you experience. Dwell on various qualities that you love. Continue to ask it to communicate.

Often I simply asked, "*Dearly Beloved, what do you have to say to me today?*" I stop thinking and hold a poised mind. I begin without having any idea or thought as to what to write. Even as the first word comes into my mind, I do not know what is coming.

This is good. The attitude of surprise is helpful and fun. The writing flows like an inner script that unfolds when attention is placed upon it. The words hold the code of our own evolution. Often they express a wisdom far beyond the rational mind.

We learn to anticipate the flow of guidance from the Essential Self, recognizing that this wisdom is our own. Essence is like a wonderful spring of living waters. It fills up daily and wants to be expressed. If it is not expressed, it will signal us by depression, disease, or addictions. The word *wants* to come forth. The inner voices want to be heard. Now is the hour of our emergence!

Neale Donald Walsch describes this process so powerfully in his *Conversations with God* books, as well as in *Friendship with God.*

Step Four: Inviting the Beloved to Take Dominion

As we contemplate the glory of the Essential Self in the Inner Sanctuary and allow it to incarnate more fully within us, the local self, weary of its compulsive behavior, becomes ever more magnetized towards the Beloved. It feels pleasure in the presence of this beneficent, loving energy that draws it forward like a baby to its mother's breast. At this stage the local, egoic personality self becomes so enchanted with the experience of its Essential Self that it freely, voluntarily, even joyfully, chooses to surrender its dominance. It invites the beloved Essential Self to enter in the whole way, to take dominion within its "household of local selves," the many sub-personalities or aspects of the local self.

There is a time in the life of a newborn infant when it gives up its resistance to existing outside the womb and starts to be more comfortable with its physical body. It opens its eyes and learns to coordinate itself—nursing, eliminating, smiling. So, too, as newly emerging Universal Humans we begin to feel more at home within ourselves, making a conscious choice to come in the whole way as who we really are.

The Story . . .

On a personal level, I began to feel the excitement and fulfillment of a passionate, inner love affair. There was the joy of homecoming, of being "mother" to myself, losing the orphaned feeling I have had since Mother's death. I realized I'd never had a motherly influence in my life from that time forward. I had been a mother of five, and wife, editor, and helper to my husband, and I had passionately loved my work and the work of so many others, but I had never regained a motherly influence in my own life. Now I was about to become mother to myself.

Finally, in my seventieth year (clearly I am very slow—I hope others do not take this long!), with the invitation from my local self to the Beloved to take dominion, "mother" came home and held the wounded child in her embrace.

In the journal, the words came:

> You have put this purpose first. You built the Inner Sanctuary and placed your attention on me. Through that attention you, local self, substantiated me. You called me in. This process requires that I, the Beloved, be invited by the local self. This is the meaning of free will. This is the meaning of personal conscious evolution. This is the substance of the transformation open to every human being on Earth. . . . I am now, by grace of your choice, to give you the reward.
>
> The reward is union with me, the ever-present, ever-loving, and all-knowing divine self of every human being on Earth. Rest your attention in me so that I can infuse you minute by minute with the elixir of the substance that actually does transubstantiate and transfigure you.

I knew a phase change in my process was occurring. First I had consciously created the space for something new to happen. Now I was experiencing that something new as the incarnation of the Beloved Self, the Essential Self, the God-self. There came a point when I realized that I, local self, wanted to fully dissolve my own identity. I no longer could stand being separate. My local self made a momentous decision.

In the Inner Sanctuary, one morning, I deliberately created a new ritual—*The Invitation to Incarnate*. I prepared the inner space and began my meditation as usual. Then solemnly, as though preparing for a marriage, I, as a local self lifting my attention to the Beloved, asked the presence of the divine to take dominion within me.

I freely gave up all domination as a local self. I realized that the illusion of separation was just that—an illusion. At that moment of invitation, like a bride preparing for the bridegroom, I declared my heart's desire for union with the Beloved. From this point on there was no turning back to the separated self, no returning to my past life of striving. The invitation to the Essential Self to take dominion is the greatest single choice I ever made since I had said yes to my vocation thirty-five years ago. I asked that the union be consummated in me eternally.

The Guidance . . .

When we make the choice to invite our Essential Self to take dominion within, we are, each of us, crossing the great divide from unconscious to conscious self-evolution. By this choice, we are transforming the nature of evolution, person by person, for evolution proceeds ever more by choice rather than by chance from this time forward.

This is the true meaning of *conscious* evolution at the personal level. Conscious evolution does not mean that we *control* evolution by human will alone. It means we humbly seek to be response-able, *able to respond*, to the deeper patterns of creation for ever-higher consciousness and greater freedom through more complex and synergistic order. It means we work with this awesome tendency in evolution, so often communicated through our inner voices urging us to transcend the limits of our personality and egoic needs.

With this choice to surrender dominion of the Essential Self, we set ourselves definitively on the gentle path to the next stage of evolution. This is the way of love. This is the *natural* birth process of Universal Humans as we cross the threshold from our self-centered, self-conscious state of being into the next phase of our development.

In the Emergence Process the local selves do not need to be forced to change; they desire it and long for their own ascension to a higher frequency because it feels so good. The pleasure principle is at work, attracting us to self-evolve, just as it attracts us to reproduce.

On this path there is no need to punish or deny the egoic, local self, whether within ourselves, personally, or in the larger world. There is forgiveness of the "sins" of the past. Sin is understood here to mean the illusion of separation from each other, from nature, and from Spirit.

As the illusion begins to fade within us, we can see that the root cause of our cruelty to one another and to other species comes from that illusion. When we actually *feel* the internal reconnection with the divine, not as an external deity but as an internal presence in resonance with the non-dual Reality, or the Godhead, equally available within all, we naturally and spontaneously experience the "other" as an Essential Self, connected to the One Supreme Reality.

At the level of essence we are all aspects of the One, whereas as individual biological egoic personalities we feel, and indeed often are, in a real struggle with one another.

From the vantage point of our evolving selves we "forgive" our own behavior as we do that of a child. We see the source of the tragedies of the human race since the Fall and correct that fault at the source where the separation occurs within ourselves. Through the process of the incarnation of the Essential Self, the separation is gradually healed, and the childlike human matures to become a conscious participant in the creation, that is, a young Universal Human.

I do not mean to imply that this is a quick and simple task, only that it is my experience that as it begins to happen to us, we naturally and spontaneously begin to love one another as part of ourselves. But until this kind of self-evolution spreads, there are still not enough people who feel this way, and therefore society, as it is now constructed, is based on separation and competition.

It is up to those who are evolving to create the social conditions and institutions that support this crossover. This is our task.

For, on the macrocosmic scale, the era of collective self-centered consciousness and local self-domination must end. Our collective local selves residing in larger entities like nation states, military/industrial establishments, and global corporations are coming to the end of their capacity to run the world by command and control, by fear and greed. They can no longer continue while billions are hungry, the environment is degrading, nuclear weapons are proliferating, the gap between the rich and poor is widening, and species are dying in the greatest cataclysm of extinction since the dinosaurs.

Our local, egoic selves are often very much like lost and wounded children who yearn to go home. This is the basis of my hope. The natural heart's desire of the separated self is reunion with the Divine. We are like individual cells in the body of a planetary system undergoing *its* crisis of birth as a whole. And the crisis of our "birth"—the new conditions which limit one form of growth in the womb of Earth—is the trigger that will hasten the inner maturation of enough of us to shift the tide of history.

In other words, I see our own emergence as a natural aspect of the planetary shift from one phase of evolution to the next. What called for extraordinary spiritual genius in the past now requires of us a more natural dedication to our unfoldment, for we are at a later stage in the developmental path of the Universal Human as members of this planetary body.

The path is to start by loving our own local selves and healing the separation between ego and essence within ourselves. This is the feminine path to the future. It is guided by the feminine within us all, both women and men, for the love of all the children of Earth, its species, and nature herself.

This is time for the Divine Mother to rise up within us and to take her rightful place as coequal co-creator with the Divine Masculine, who has so brilliantly given us the power to create and destroy but who can no longer guide that power for us alone.

Let the thinking layer of Earth sound the clarion call of its feminine voices of co-creation! Let the feminine co-creator, who understands these new powers, join with the masculine co-creator, to lovingly and ethically guide our new capacities to heal and evolve our world!

Invitation to Incarnate

When the local self has become magnetized to the Beloved and is released sufficiently from its compulsiveness, you are ready for the ritual, Invitation to Incarnate. In your meditation, prepare the Inner Sanctuary for a special event. Place your attention in the household of local selves, the ones who have been asking, seeking, and attempting to follow guidance. Raise your consciousness upward toward the Essential Self and invite the Beloved to take dominion within the household of all the selves—the anxious, the fearful, the driven.

Even deeper, invite the Beloved to radiate its presence upon the primal source of all fear—the great fall, fault, or chasm within, which is the illusion of separation of the human from the divine. Declare that you want to cast the light of truth upon the shadow, the unconscious source of fear within yourself. Ask for a complete union of the human and the divine within yourself. In this moment, ego invites essence to come in the whole way, and the next stage of incarnation proceeds.

If possible, give yourself extra time. Take long walks in nature. Be present with yourself, as though it were your wedding day. Feel the presence of the Beloved, now freely invited to consummate the union. Be poised and expectant with a "beginner's mind," no thoughts, no agenda, just innocence, openness, and love.

Radiate the Presence of the Essential Self within Yourself

Normally, in our interactions with others, we radiate our best thoughts and intentions outward and receive energy back from others' responses to what we have given. In support of the Emergence Process, however, we can practice a different kind of interaction, which is consciously radiating the internal presence, the Beloved, inwardly rather than outwardly.

Whenever a local self acts up, feels stress, hurt, anger, anxiety, or fear, we can learn to radiate the inner presence upon that wounded self. This radiance actually calms the egoic personality and gives us time to listen to the problem, whatever it may be. (In later steps of the Emergence Process, we see how this also gives us time to begin consciously to educate the many local selves.)

Continue to Put This Purpose First

Remember the attraction for the Beloved and keep returning to the contemplation of the glory of the divine essence.

Journal

Moral Inventory/Offering Up

Prepare for the Beloved to enter into dominion by taking a moral inventory and cleaning house. Ask, "What do I not want to have happening in my life any more?" (In my case, it was my compulsive, workaholic fear of failure.) Record your answers. Realize that when the Beloved takes dominion, those experiences will no longer be dominant; our contracted local selves are lifted up and transformed.

At this stage we come to the realization that the local self, like an alcoholic, can no longer handle our life, yet there is a higher power that can, and we are ready to turn our lives over to that higher power, our Essential Self, connected incorruptibly to Source. In preparation for the Invitation, we take a moral inventory and prepare each aspect of our personalities to release their illusion of separation.

Step Five: The Bliss of Union of the Human and Divine

The Beloved has been invited home and is now taking dominion within the household of local selves. In this next stage, for the first time, the Beloved takes the initiative and invites the local selves to come up unto it. With their ready acceptance, the local selves are lifted up unto the Beloved. They enter a chamber of the heart, and there, in the field of love, they experience the great reward—the Bliss of Union of the Human and Divine. We are freed in that instant from our illusion of separation from our Essential Self. Our divine essence is experienced personally as the creator within, the source and life pulse of the great creating process, animating the local self as its instrument of expression in the world—as a young Universal Human.

Just as the newborn rests blissfully in its mother's arms after the trauma of birth, so we experience the bliss of union with our essential, divine self. The bliss of union deepens the frequencies of the Essential Self throughout the whole body/mind, accelerating the alchemy of our transubstantiation and incarnation.

The Story . . .

As my own Emergence Process continued, the inner love affair deepened. I arose with excitement every morning and hastened into the protected space of the Inner Sanctuary. There, almost daily now, I experienced a tremendous opening, an infusion of love coming in waves that flooded both my heart and my solar plexus region. What had been a somewhat flashing type of joy in the past was now intensified. It felt like a sun was shining inside me, not just coming and going.

To hold this new experience, I formed a deeper chamber within the Inner Sanctuary and called it the "Rose Chamber of Union of the Human and the Divine." In this new space, I experienced a glowing, rose-colored light with a misty quality—almost like a morning dew—which I could feel on my face as I entered in.

To enhance the mood and evoke the tones of the higher self, I played the "multidimensional music" of Jacotte Chollet, which creates a state of unification and expansion of consciousness in which the two hemispheres of the brain are connected and synchronized. (See references on page 176.)

As I remained in the Chamber, the rose-colored light gently permeated the density of my body, infusing itself deeply through every part. It felt as though the frequency of my body was shifting vibrationally and being transmuted into light.

The unconditional love of the Beloved embraced me so deeply that there was no fear, no anxiety, no death. Nothing but light and bliss and joy. This experience, so often described by mystics, was happening now through union with an ultrapersonal self—my own Beloved essence—rather than an impersonal self, a non-dual Reality, or external deity.

In that instant in the Rose Chamber, I released my identity as the local self. "I" disappeared into the light, absorbed by it and remaining in it for some time. When the experience was complete, I felt that I would never leave the Rose Chamber because the frequencies had imprinted themselves on me.

When I emerged from the experience and entered into what had been my local self persona, that familiar persona was no longer there. My local self had been transmuted by a higher frequency which had released it from its delusional separation. It felt as though the local self disappeared and then reappeared again but was now transformed by the frequency of that rose-colored light, the essence of the Beloved.

When the local self, or multiple versions of local self, reappeared, they were vibrating with a new frequency gained through the bliss of union. I felt lighter. Their density was gone. I could see their positive aspects. The anxious one was gently giving me energy to fulfill my work, urging me onward. The local self that feared failure was asking me to be excellent, while the one that was judgmental became discerning. Yet all of them seemed like facets of the Beloved, rather than their fragmented, negative former selves.

In the bliss of union, the local self gives up the kind of desire that leads to attachment because its desire is already met through the union with the Beloved. Then comes forth another kind of desire—a life-enhancing, happiness-generating desire. It is the desire to self-express and self-actualize through creative expression.

This form of desire guides us as a compass of joy through the density of daily life in the material world. The desire to bring essence into form is vital to our full emergence as Universal Humans. It is the process whereby we transform ourselves and the world.

I found that my compulsive desire to "get the job done" was becoming a creative flow of Essential Self-expression. I entered a flow state wherein desire no longer felt personal but was rather the expression of universal creativity flowing through me in this particular form.

Shortly after this experience, these words flowed forth into my journal:

> I am always with you. I will never leave you. Whenever you are in pain, when you feel the nameless anxiety, driveness, and fear that you will not complete the task, stop, breathe, and I will calm your agitated self. I will do more. Since I am now taking dominion within your being, I will take the initiative. I will radiate my presence. I will breathe you up unto me so that your heaviness becomes my lightness; your fear is comforted through our union. This now, I, Essential Self, commit to you. I am no longer the distant presence to be called upon in your journal. I am the passionate lover of you, my local self.

My heart melted with joy.

As I spent more and more time in the Rose Chamber, I could feel the Beloved residing there unconditionally, regardless of what I was doing in my daily life. Whenever my local self reappeared to drive a car or write a book, make a telephone call or give a speech, the frequencies I experienced in the Rose Chamber were with me.

When I interacted with others, I noticed I had a very different effect than I was used to. This new local self, united and infused with the Beloved, I found, could transmit bliss. People recognized the bliss and would often ask me what was different.

This surprised me, because I wasn't intentionally doing anything different. But when I replied, "I've been experiencing the bliss of union in the Rose Chamber," they would say, "That's where I want to be!" I would then respond, using the same language the Beloved had used with me, "Come up unto the Beloved within yourself."

People were very quickly lifted up, because the field had been established in me, and the readiness was there in them. It's contagious! I found that I could be to other peoples' local selves what I, as the Beloved, was learning to be to my own. The Beloved does for others what it does for its own local self. The Beloved doesn't care whose selves they are—all are uplifted!

When I shared my experiences of emergence with friends, I found that many of them were having similar experiences. I realized that I was not alone, that in this process of mapping my own emergence, I was discovering a developmental path that has generic elements.

As in a biological organism, each of us is unique, and yet there are common stages we all pass through. In sharing our emergence experiences among ourselves, we act as the Darwin of an evolving humanity. He went to the Galapagos Islands to study the turtles. Now, we are the turtles! We are the species being studied in the hidden act of mutating! We are the data we need. We echo back to each other our essential selves. We fall in love with one another at the essence level. This experience vastly accelerates our own integration and emergence.

The Guidance . . .

As we undergo this next step in the Emergence Process, we are awakened to the memory of an earlier bliss of union that we all share. For this is not a new experience but rather one we are retrieving, a very ancient knowing, seeded within ourselves at the origin of our creation.

Many of us have touched upon this memory in intuitive flashes of oneness, moments of ecstatic reunion with the whole of which we are vital parts, confirming that we all arise out of one universal process of creation. Mystics and saints have inspired us with descriptions of the ecstasy of union with the divine, and most of our religions were founded upon this experience in all its diversity.

Each of us knows this experience personally, as we were conceived in the bliss of union of two seeds of life joined in the embrace of our parents and have experienced the ecstasy of sexuality ourselves.

Far from being self-indulgent or selfish, the experience of ecstasy is the incentive and condition that leads us to our full integration as Universal Humans and so is vital to the survival and fulfillment of humanity. Here, the Emergence Process deepens, for, as we know, life can be an ordeal as challenges arise and difficulties appear.

What gives us the incentive to overcome obstacles, to climb every mountain, to swim across every river, is the carrot of the bliss of union held out before us. It is our heart's desire, our soul's motivation. It is not abstract; we feel it whole-bodily. The local self finds its heart's desire is met in this union of the human and divine. Bliss is its reward; it needs no other.

Create a Chamber of Union
of the Human and Divine

When you feel ready, following your own inner guidance, set aside a special day (as you did for the Invitation to Incarnation ritual) for the Beloved to create the Rose Chamber and invite the local selves up unto itself. You can invent your own rituals, images, ceremonies, and meditations for this event. I am sharing the ones that I love, hoping that you will add wonderful new ones, and then share them with me, and with each other. Here is the ritual I have used:

Prepare the Inner Sanctuary once again. Special flowers, music, candle, incense may be chosen. Sit quietly and focus your attention on the Beloved. Allow the divine presence to come into the heart and to create there a Rose Chamber filled with rose-colored light (or whatever color most attracts you). This heart light is blissful, the radiant presence of the divine within you.

Feel the Beloved residing at the center of the Rose Chamber, infusing the Chamber with its presence. Allow the local selves to ascend into the rosy light, floating within the field. Experience the Essential Self as a radiant presence, glowing and emanating light. Feel your vibration increase. Your local selves are now ascending in vibration, merging and becoming one with the Beloved.

In its presence, the local selves are repatterning, attuning to the higher frequency of the Essential Self. Their knots of concern are dissolving, their density is lightening, and their weary selves are being renewed.

The voice of the Beloved is speaking within, now no longer hovering and signaling from afar but alive within your body/mind. Let the local selves merge with the light. Feel the bliss of union of the human and the divine.

Dwell in the Rose Chamber as long as you can. Return to the Chamber throughout the day. The continual experience of the bliss of union stabilizes the fusion process of the essential and local selves. The unitive flashes of the past become the union experience of the present, as we are naturally normalized in a gentle state of bliss, a gentle ecstatic experience.

In the Rose Chamber, the vibrational field of the Beloved penetrates deep within the cellular level, like an internal healer whose hands are vibrating with the frequencies needed to restore and regenerate life. Notice that the alchemical process is accelerating. Currents of joy, fields of bliss lift the vibrational field within you.

The longer we stay in the Rose Chamber, the more wonderful becomes the rest of the day. A rosy glow from the Rose Chamber lingers on, infusing daily life with an all-pervading joy. The local selves purr like kittens. They want more of it! Instead of trying to get us to do something outside ourselves, they are now calling us to return to the Rose Chamber! Their deepest heart's desire is gratified.

It has always been for union, whether it is with the mother, with the lover, with God. Now, "God" is found permanently residing as the Essential Self of each newly born Universal Human. "Heaven," or joy, is our natural state at this next level of evolution.

Also, the longer we stay in the Rose Chamber of Union, the more sustainable becomes the native state of happiness. This is not a mind-blowing ecstasy but rather a gentle infusion of peace, warmth, and contentment. In the Rose Chamber, we participate in the world-changing truth of all mystics: *The Kingdom of Heaven is within you.* It is heavenly in the Rose Chamber.

Follow the Compass of Joy

This spiritual joy can be summoned by fixing the experience into our nervous system such that it can be replayed at will with a flick of attention. Simply remember the bliss, and the needle of your attention swings immediately toward it. Instead of focusing on a problem or pain, concentrate on bliss and joy.

Make a clear internal decision when you feel local self arise. Attract its attention to the Beloved. Firmly, decisively, shift your focus to the Rose Chamber. The local self will recede, as warmth infuses the body/mind. We are learning to orchestrate our own inner reality as young Universal Humans.

Presence the Radiance of the Beloved

Moment by moment, during this blessed period of time, keep your attention on the Beloved and infuse your body/mind with its presence. It is an inner healer filled with warm, relaxing, harmonizing light bathing the weary, wounded, separated selves. Just as self-consciousness must have been difficult to remember for early humans in the animal world; so cosmic, universal consciousness is hard for us to remember in the midst of the self-centered world. We flicker in and out like flames in the wind.

Be Rigorous

Every time you feel the old patterns of anxiety, fear, or nervousness, *stop*. *Breathe*. Focus on the Beloved and allow that presence to lift you up. We need to slow down to accomplish our rendezvous with destiny. Our inner state of being is largely our choice. We are at cause of our own experience, not at effect of circumstances in the world. This is basic metaphysical teaching practiced here for the specific purpose of incarnating as Universal Humans.

Cultivate Resonance

As much as possible, stay within yourself or with the "two or more" friends who can resonate with and mirror back to you your Essential Self. Resonance means resounding, echoing back and affirming the highest in one another. It occurs when our hearts are open and we share deeply from our essential selves in an environment of safety and non-judgment.

To reinforce the inner experience, it is highly desirable to seek out communion with two or more others—to expand the Inner Sanctuary to include others. This environment of resonance is created in circles with processes of attunement, deep sharing, attention to the heart, and non-judgment of one another.

Do not hesitate to put out the call to others. Share your experience. See whose heart it touches. Others are waiting for you as you are waiting for them. Each time you share your experience it deepens in you. The word becomes flesh when spoken. At this stage we vitally need kindred others to stimulate and recognize ourselves. Have the courage to share your story and experience. Thus you become a guide to awaken the guide within others.

Form an Emergence Circle

If you feel so moved, invite two or more friends (if you have not already done so) to share the Emergence Process with you. Arranging this is simple. Set aside sacred time. Create sacred space, flowers, candles, incense, music. Sit in a circle. To begin, be silent. Do a meditation or attunement, evoking the Essential Self in each person. Then do a brief "check in," describing how each of you is feeling right now. Share with one another exactly where you are in your own emergence, offering gentle encouragement to one another.

It is not, however, a therapy session. The circle is a space to experience spiritual intimacy, non-judgment, unconditional love, and resonance. Develop your own rituals. When you are finished, close with a blessing. This process acts as a nurturing "birthing field" for young Universal Humans. (*The Co-creator's Handbook: An Experiential Guide to Discovering and Fulfilling Your Soul's Purpose,* by Carolyn Anderson and Katharine Roske, is a marvelous guide and is especially designed as a companion to *Emergence.*)

Journal

Write from the Bliss

Place yourself in the Rose Chamber of Union. Feel the bliss. Lift up your local selves unto you. Feel their ecstasy. Allow the beloved to write to the local selves, its poems of love, its songs of praise, its voice of compassion. Bask in the ecstasy of union as long as you can every day. Record your experiences and internal messages.

Childhood

Step Six: Shifting Our Identity

At a point in its development, the infant becomes a child. If the first period of life has gone well, and the infant has fully experienced its union with its mother, it can now internalize that love and reach out into the world with confidence. So, as we feel the bliss of union in our infancy as Universal Humans, the maturation process accelerates. A new identity emerges, born out of the fusion of the Beloved and the local selves. The young Universal Human emerges.

We enter our Childhood, not as the Essential Self alone, but as the Essential Self expressing through its personality self. We are becoming a self-governing, sovereign person in the world, albeit, still a limited and protected world. In Childhood we come together as our integrated selves, learning as co-creators to socialize, to follow the authority of the inner teacher, to educate our local selves, and to play at co-creating with one another. We enter a "kindergarten of the godlings."

The Story . . .

I continued to spend time in the Inner Sanctuary, experiencing the bliss of union as dominion of the Beloved took hold. I was already familiar with the Beloved; she has been my companion all my life. Behind the curtain of my consciousness, she had been sending signals. Now, the curtains were parting to reveal this familiar presence as my Essential Self, visible and recognized at last. I was flooded with gratitude and joy.

The inner being that I so loved, that had lifted me beyond my biological life and brought me to the point of emergence, is ME. I had to get used to this identity.

I am aware of the specific moment in time when the phase change from Infancy to Childhood occurred for me. It was an instant of profound self-recognition of what had always been so, but only now was I able to realize it. It required a conscious effort on my part to shift the "I" of identity—where I reside in my internal state of being—from the one who was asking to the one who knows.

In the Inner Sanctuary, I had already been practicing remembering the presence of the Beloved, but now I placed the "I" of identity in that beloved presence. This I did as a conscious act of will and attention. As I made the inner shift of identity, I could feel the vibrations within me change. Warmth and joy flooded my being. I found I could exert choice as to my "inner weather." I could dispel the clouds and bring in the sunlight with a flick of attention upon the Beloved as myself.

To anchor the shift, I spoke out loud and then wrote down a set of declarative statements, including: "I am the Guide who's been guiding. I am the voice I've been hearing. I am the Beloved that I have loved. I am the Universal Human I've been preparing to birth. As that, I am here, present now, in every cell of my being."

I recorded these words in my journal and spoke them out loud as part of my practice. Then I felt the words become flesh as they incarnated and filled me with their radiance. I consumed the words. They were alive in me.

As this process continued, I realized that, as the Beloved, I had been hovering, suspended in space, because I didn't want to come into the flesh the whole way. I was afraid of losing my vision, of being trapped in materiality. I had signaled to my local selves to do more than they could possibly do. I remained aloof and put all the responsibility on them for carrying out my signals, which they could only intuit. I sent my motivational signals and guidance, then I disappeared.

Now, the reverse was happening. As I placed my "I" of identity in the Beloved and raised my local selves up unto me, my local selves disappeared and reappeared as aspects of the Essential Self. After my identity had gone through the phase shift, I was willing to take responsibility as the Beloved for the full incarnation in all aspects of my being.

The affirmations I had created as positive declarations, both written and spoken, were now taking hold. I experienced an expanded sense of inner knowing. "I," Essential Self, know everything "we," the family of local selves, need to know. I had already found that when I asked, a wise response always came. Now I realize that I am the wise one who has been responding!

A tremendous sense of inner self-confidence arose as I realized that this informed and informing self is always omnipresent and omniscient as far as my own requirements are concerned. There is nothing that I have ever asked the Beloved that she did not have a wise response for. Now that I have recognized myself as the Beloved, I realize that I have the wisdom and can assist others in the world.

This inner wisdom is always transmitting, and I am that transmitter. I am not an isolated I, but an I that is integrated *upward* with Source, *inward* with the essence of others, and *onward* with the evolutionary impulse of creation toward higher consciousness and greater freedom. But it requires a poised mind, deep centering, and precise focus to stabilize the new comprehensive identity.

My practice over the last forty-four years of recording the inner voice and following its commands now took a new turn. I had shifted the locus of my conscious mind from the local to the beloved self, from ego to essence, and from that vantage point "I," Essential Self, incarnated in all levels of my being. I did it deliberately, in slow motion, so I could feel it thoroughly. What began to express was a new, integrated identity—the Universal Human.

In my journal I began, as the Beloved, to address the local selves as I practiced holding my I of identity as my Essential Self. My practice is to consciously shift from listening and being guided by the inner voice, to speaking as the voice, to being the self that is one with Universal Mind. In this way, I learn to act as the personal essence incarnate with my ego in service to my Essential Self.

As I write, the very shift of attention sends a vibration of joy through my nervous system. I feel stabilized, grounded through my hand and my pen and the ink as the words flow spontaneously onto paper. I am now writing the words into my flesh and blood rather than simply onto the paper to be later followed by a separated and dutiful local self. I maintain my identity as Guide through writing to the local self, the guided. The journal writing changed:

Dearly Beloved,

I am now the Universal Human who is already here, full, complete, gently instructing the local self. Local Self! I want you to fully know that the being writing this is me, the me you were told to become. I am not writing this as a Christ voice. I am writing this as Barbara, a Universal Human who is in the same domain as those higher voices you thought were writing through you before. I am, by my full intention and attention, that self in this form writing this now.

Local self, I ask you to release, let go, dissolve, fulfill yourself in me as me. The way I can best assist you is by clearly writing to you as the Me, with my relationship with higher beings secured—still in touch with higher domains of reality I draw from, and through that with the Designing Intelligence, and through that with Meta-universe, Ground of Being, Void, Field of All Possibilities, Pure Awareness, the Godhead.

"I" am the Universal Human. "You" are the still-maturing local self, asking, seeking, fearing, excited, and sad.

I am present now in this writing. I am the one writing. The way we move toward our reward—our integration as a unified being—is for me to hold the field consciously while you, local self, ask me questions. My goal with you, beloved local self, is your full acceptance and fulfillment of your mission through your ecstatic union with me and our unified communion and communication in the world as that.

You are to spend longer times protected from the old thought patterns of the local self until you can stabilize more permanently. The alchemical process is arrested, stopped, whenever an extraneous thought gets your attention. When the thought captures your attention, you collapse and feel the sinking of the beloved field. It is the collapse of the wave—the non-local field you are in—to the particle, the one specific thought that holds you at the moment. Yet you are a co-creator; you are to be supremely active once again in the world. This is your initiation.

The key now is to use profound affirmations continually all day: *I am the Universal Human at one with all that is.*

At this point in my process, I continued to write in my journal as the Beloved, recording my affirmations and declarations, and returning as often as possible to the Inner Sanctuary to visit the Rose Chamber and experience the bliss of union. But even though I had experienced a profound shift of identity in my Emergence Process, I still found it easy to forget who I am as essence. The retraining of my nervous system must overcome more than 50,000 years of programming in the early phase of self-conscious *Homo sapiens*, so I am patient and humble.

When I forget who I am, or feel discouraged, it helps me to recall the whole story of creation. I remind myself that this is not a neutral universe but one with a direction toward higher consciousness and greater freedom through more synergistic order—a fifteen billion-year trend. I "surf the spiral" in my imagination. (See "Wheel of Co-Creation" diagram on page 177.) I feel its irresistible tendency to overcome every obstacle to more life. I am tapping into the "grace," which is that added energy beyond human will that comes from the process of creation itself, from God.

The same force that brought us from sub-atomic particles to the present is the grace at work to evolve us now. The grace I feel is that overwhelming tide of creativity forever forming the universe in all its dimensions.

We stand at the very tip of the spiral of evolution. We reach our antennae way back in the past to remember the whole story of our creation. And at the same time, we penetrate deeply into the *now*, the present, to drink from the well of the ever-present source of creation. And we cast our vision forward to experience the reality of our own emergence. Through imagining ourselves fulfilled, we lodge the hook in the right crevice up the side of Mt. Evolution to secure us as we climb forward to actual fulfillment of what we envision and choose.

The Guidance . . .

A profound phase shift ushers in this Childhood as Universal Humans. In Infancy surrendered to the Essential Self and invi dominion, but we had not yet emerged as t   ..te- grated identity. Now, we undergo a transitio.. in which there is a definitive crossing-over from that egoic self to the Essential Self and the formation of a new integrated iden- tity. At this first step, we prepare to move from the inner world of incarnation to the outer world of integration, and eventually, full co-creation.

The shift of identity from ego to essence at this stage of development marks the recognition of who we really are, the moment of self-revelation. The veil of separation between ego and essence is rent asunder. We realize that we are that inner voice that has been communicating with us. We are the Guide who has been guiding us. We are the Essential Self, the Beloved we have worshipped—and experienced—from afar. We are fusing the transforming ego and incarnating essence as an integrated, whole Universal Human.

Almaas describes this shift beautifully in *Essence* (1986):

> The shift of identity from personality to essence is nothing but the realization of the true self, the high self of essence. Practical action becomes the action of true being. There is efficiency, economy, simplicity, direct- ness. One fully lives in the world but is constantly con- nected to the Beyond, the Supreme Reality.
>
> This integration of all aspects of essence into a new and personal synthesis is the pearl beyond price. When the pearl is first born, it is usually not complete; it is the essential child. It is born as a personal kernel. Then it integrates all of the aspects of essence into its very

bstance. . . . There is balance, completeness, harmony, fullness, contentment.

All inner compulsion will be gone, for the person is realized, and the realization is based on fullness, richness, and value as a mature being. . . . The station of the pearl beyond price is so significant because it is not a matter of a state of consciousness or being; it is rather the condition of the actualization of one's realization in one's life.

Life becomes a process of creative discovery. . . . The ego does not need to work any more. The creative process happens on its own.

That which seemed to come from beyond is now experienced as incarnated within. The Essential Self's presence has been received within the household of selves as what we call the "Lord" in some traditions, echoing the words of the old hymn, "Mine eyes have seen the glory of the coming of the Lord." Now the glory we see is the Lord recognized—not above us, but in us, as us.

There have been great individuals throughout all of history who have made this shift of identity to incarnate as the divine. Jesus said, "If you have seen me, you have seen the Father," and, "The Father and I are one." Such Great Ones founded the major religions of the world and have been the ears and eyes of evolving humanity.

Now the very consciousness that awakened in the Great Ones of the past is ready to incarnate in us as a new norm, when we "Put This Purpose First"—not because we are better or wiser than those who came before but because we are the generation born when the whole planetary system is integrating as a whole and awakening its members to the next stage of our evolution, both self and social.

During the gestation phase of the developmental path, we were attracted and attuned to our spiritual ancestors, those particular teachers most compatible with our meta-physical type. When we go through the shift of identity, we don't stop attuning to and learning from teachers and masters. We draw from them ever more deeply during our process. But ultimately, our relationship to God changes from child to joint heir, from passive recipient to active participant, from creature to co-creator. We become able to respond to the deeper patterns of creation through the integration of the human and divine within ourselves.

That inner union provides a receptivity to the larger design, and our desire to create provides the motivation. We recognize ourselves and others as newly born Universal Humans. This is, I believe, the next stage of human evolution. This is the human being that has been heralded and foreshadowed for eons by the great teachers that came before us to pave the way.

With the shift of identity, we move from witness consciousness to causal consciousness. As the witness, we place our "I"—our being state—of identity in the perspective of observer: "I" am not my body; "I" am not my mind; "I" am not my emotions. I am simply witnessing the ever-changing phenomenal world.

Once we have shifted our identity from ego to essence, we are no longer a witness of the phenomenal world but a co-creator of the phenomenal world. In this new perspective, we actually experience that our larger "mind" or consciousness is causing our reality. The experience of personal freedom shifts from a sense of individual, separated will to a sense of surrender into a larger design which feels like it is our own.

On the macrocosmic level, the full intention of creation is arising with this profound shift in our species. Creation is triumphant in its magnificent struggle to evolve from cosmic dust to cosmic consciousness, embodied at last in cosmic humans who know they are at one with the process of creation. In a deep sense, this is a homecoming for God and humans together.

If the intention of God is to reproduce godlings, if the intention of the creator is to evolve co-creators, if the tendency in evolution is to create beings capable of co-evolution with nature and co-creation with Spirit, then God (by whatever name it is called) and humans can celebrate together the next stage in the fulfillment of this highest purpose. This intention has been manifesting for billions of years through the emergence of life out of pre-life, human life out of animal life, and now, the emergence of Universal Humanity out of ego-centered humanity.

Our evolution has been an awesome journey of fifteen billion years. Every entity that ever moved or swam or crawled or flew, every being that lived to reproduce itself, all the vast numbers of species now extinct and presently living, who invented the amazing capability which we have inherited as our eyes, our ears, our organs, our very atoms, molecules and cells—all of those preceding us are represented in our emergence now. We bow down in awe and gratitude for the past. Without all that came before us, none of us would be awakening now!

With this profound shift, we have arrived symbolically at the eighth day of creation. In Genesis, on the seventh day, God rested and saw that "it was good." The image of a creator God as a sole and separated entity is now complete, finished. On the eighth day, humanity awakens and we realize *we are* co-creating as expressions of the divine.

As young Universal Humans, we enter a new beginning, the second chapter in the history of the world, the first age of conscious evolution, when we participate in the process of evolution consciously, by choice. It could be called co-genesis.

The process of shifting our identity certainly requires no less from us than the training an athlete must go through for the Olympics. It requires total commitment, daily practice, coaching from others, self-observation, intentionality, and grace.

Shift Your *"I"* of Identity to the Beloved

When you check within yourself, ask, "Where does the 'I' reside?" Does it reside in the local self that receives a higher voice, or does it reside in the higher voice that communicates to the local selves? If you are residing in the local personality self, when you feel ready, deliberately shift your attention into the Beloved. Practice placing the I of identity—the locus of your deepest sense of where the "I" is—in and as the Beloved. Use the feedback signals of joy, peace, love, and freedom as signs that you have made the inner shift. See how long you can hold these feelings until they become not a fleeting moment of grace but a state of being, even a "station," as Almaas calls it, because these qualities are recognized as the essence of yourself rather than a passing feeling.

Be the Beloved

Now practice putting your "I of Identity" into yourself as Guide by asking, "Local self, do you have any questions for me?" Sit in the presence of yourself as *that*. When the local self presents you with a dilemma, such as time running out, or lack of self-esteem, or feeling rejected, jealous, or competitive, don't try to fix the situation by offering a solution. Instead, lift the local questioner up unto yourself, re-experience the bliss of union, and release it. Let it speak to you. Then allow the Beloved to respond spontaneously without preconception. In this way, we learn spontaneous direct thinking, direct knowing, direct speaking. We gain spontaneous access to essential wisdom. We become the Word. The Word becomes flesh in us. The Word is the Word of direct knowing.

We don't want to confuse this kind of self-expression with "channeling," which occurs when people put aside their local self and feel an external entity coming through them. In the Emergence Process, the entity is the essence of the person. If we want to incarnate fully, we cannot have hovering entities telling local selves what to do.

This does not mean that there are no higher beings, or even that they might not communicate directly with us. But at this stage, the best practice is to focus on incarnating the highest wisdom and accepting the fact that we are that wisdom ourselves.

Affirmations

Select your own affirmations, use them in your meditative time in the Inner Sanctuary, and repeat them throughout the day. Whenever your thoughts veer downward toward an old problem, worrying a wound aimlessly, consciously shift your attention to the affirmation. Let the affirmations become your mantras and experience incarnating these qualities in your being. Feel your presence substantiating. For example:

> *I AM love.*
> *I AM wisdom.*
> *I AM faith.*
> *I AM courage.*
> *I AM power.*
> *I AM patience.*
> *I AM surrender.*

Maintain the Self-Remembering Presence

Get used to the "is-ness" of yourself as the Beloved. Place your attention in that Essential Self, resting there in calmness as you go through your day. Sometimes it feels to me like an inner smile radiating out, warming myself, and all who pass by. It is the kind of smile you see on the face of the Dalai Lama—not because things are going well in Tibet, but because his inner presence is at peace, he is aware of the impermanence of the phenomenal world, he is compassionate and kind. He practices "initiatory love." His is not the kind of love you give when someone loves you, but the love you initiate from your own essence unconditionally, because that is who you are as a Universal Human.

Speak Out Loud as the Beloved

To get started, it is very helpful to tape your own inner voice, the "Voice of the Beloved." Practice writing in your journal as the Beloved, then reading what you write into a recorder. Place classical or baroque music behind it, like Pachebel's *Canon in D*. This tempo facilitates superlearning and memory.

Turn on your own recorded inner voice as you are going to sleep. When the voice of the Beloved speaks out loud in the household of selves, the cells awaken to their next phase of life. This is the signal they need to begin their cycle of regeneration and full expression of latent capacities.

Our cells are like seeds in spring, awaiting the warmth of the sun and the moisture of the rain. That sun and rain pours forth from the voice of the Beloved. Let it be heard in the land of your selves. The alchemical process of metamorphosis is accelerated through the vibration of the voice of the Beloved. Behold! We are experiencing a mystery, and we are being changed now.

Inner Voice Dialogue

Speak as the Beloved in your Emergence Circles or in other small groups of others willing to emerge with you as their guide. This is a new form of conversation for emerging Universal Humans. The voice of the Beloved needs now to be spoken with one another. This creates a magnetic field of resonance between the two or more. The voice tone of each person stimulates the inner knowing of the others. Thoughts come forth that are deeper than the intellectual, analytical kind. They are thoughts resonant with direct knowing. They are like poetry and scripture coming from within us.

If at all possible, tape record these conversations among the Beloved and listen to them again and again. The combination of journaling, focused attention, inner voice dialogues, and speaking out loud as the Beloved helps to secure the state of grace.

Journal

Write as the Beloved. Pick a mantra such as "I am a Universal Human" or "I am the Beloved." Place your I of identity in that essence. Allow the voice to write as itself. Do not edit or think. As you write, experience how "the word becomes flesh." You are not channeling a higher entity. You are the higher entity yourself.

Make a special section for the concentrated voice of the Beloved. Share it with kindred souls. Read it during times of sharing with friends.

When you, Beloved self, give guidance, let the local selves arise and come to you with their burdens and their pain. Be there for all the selves. This will also make you a beneficent healer of others' local selves, once you learn to do it for your own.

Cumulative Meditation

You have come a long distance in your Emergence Process, and it may be helpful to recapture the entire process through a meditation that touches all previous steps. The following is one you may want to record and play back for meditation, if you find it useful:

> I enter the Inner Sanctuary that resides forever in my heart. I am at peace, I am at rest, I am fully protected and safe. In this sacred space, I place my attention on the Beloved that I am, dwelling in that brilliance and beauty of the Presence of the Beloved, experiencing the qualities that I most particularly choose to express today.

> I remember my invitation to the Beloved to take full dominion within the household of the separated selves. I remember the experience of that incarnation as the Beloved entered in at my invitation, infusing into every fiber of my being her divine radiance for the very first time. I experience bliss in the rose-colored field of union of the human and the divine.

> I enter this field now, allowing the radiance to penetrate every cell and molecule of my being, as I feel myself disappear in the radiant field, losing all my boundaries of separation. I fade away and no longer exist, losing my self-consciousness, becoming one with the Beloved. In that oneness, I am one with all. I am infused with this bliss of union. My cells remember the pattern of their own regeneration and life evermore abundant.

> I remain in the Rose Chamber for as long as my heart desires. When I am ready, I re-appear no longer a separated self. I am the eyes and ears and hands and feet of the Beloved. I am a Universal Human. I have come home now.

Step Seven: Transferring Authority

As a child matures beyond infancy, it can no longer react in a totally self-centered way. It must learn to behave in the world, to follow its parents' and teachers' guidance. The young Universal Human does the same, but in the Emergence Process we learn that the parental authority is within us, as our essential divine essence.

Until recently, the beloved self has remained aloof, signaling but not fully incarnating. The local selves were often left on their own, like latchkey children, trying to serve the higher purpose, but disconnected from their source of power, or acting without the intimate, felt presence of a loving parent. Now, as the process of incarnating continues, the Essential Self becomes proactive and is willing to be the genuine authority within the household of selves. This inner authority does not impose any form of punishment, guilt or asceticism, for our local selves are becoming willing disciples of the Essential Self within.

The Story . . .

As I began to take authority as the Beloved, my local self let me know it didn't trust me to be fully present. In the past, I'd hovered and signaled from afar, leaving my local self on its own to complete the job without the advantage of my full presence and incarnation.

Local self had been put up to huge tasks through inspiring signals, such as, "Go tell the story of the birth of a Universal Humanity," or "Work for the transformation of the American presidency" (which I did by running and succeeding to have my name placed in nomination for the vice president of the United States on the Democratic ticket—proposing a Peace Room in the White House to be as sophisticated as a war room).

But I, Beloved, had not been fully incarnated. I had left the local selves to carry the burden of my commands given from afar without the energy and love that I infuse in them with my full radiant presence in the present. My local selves suffered from the illusion of separation from me, which was the source of their anxiety and driven behavior.

This acceptance of inner responsibility and authority on the part of the Essential Self was clearly the next part of my process to accept the full power that I am. As I entered this stage, I had shifted my identity from local to Essential Self, and was ready to transfer authority from the local selves who prod and push, to the Beloved who literally takes the "throne" in the kingdom of heaven within. I realized that my external work in the world must now spring from the internal seat of authority, from the point of power of the Essential Self.

However, in the process, I discovered I didn't have a strong internal authority. My own inner parents needed maturing. In life, I'd had an overly dominant, demanding, very competitive, and successful father and a beautiful but submissive mother, underdeveloped because she had died so young. Within me, these two archetypes, my masculine and feminine aspects, were divided and immature, undermining my internal authority.

My father was irritable and brilliant, shouting at his employees, frightening his children and wife. I can still feel his personality acting out through me whenever I am flooded with irritation. But I learned to hate authority because of how my father used it and as a result have always resisted becoming the head of anything, not wanting the responsibility.

To strengthen my inner masculine, I envisioned the father I wish I'd had as being within myself. He listens carefully to my fears and desires. He has worldly wisdom and can take my hand and show a better way to achieve my heart's desire. He is powerful, creative, and infuses me with the energy of the inner masculine.

My feminine aspect also began to take shape. My own mother had never had a chance to mature, dying at thirty-three of breast cancer. I remember her as exquisitely beautiful, smiling shyly while my father ranted and raged, often in jest or love, but like a great bear in contrast to a gazelle. When I asked her in my prayers many years later, Why did you die? the answer I received was, "I was so angry at your father, but I couldn't express myself, so I died."

My own inner mother was arrested in her development, had never grown and matured. And in my own life, I had failed to be the nurturer to myself.

I started to bring forth the inner mother. I asked myself: Could I have a garden again? Could I open my recipe books which I hadn't looked at for thirty-five years? Could I simply enjoy myself in my home? Could I even have a home? I'd lost that side of my life.

I began to pay attention to the grieving girl within me who was motherless, always subtly seeking her mother in the most inappropriate people! I called her up unto me as the Divine Daughter. I embraced and nurtured her with all the mother love I had so yearned for. I noticed that my chronic feeling of loneliness began to disappear.

When I returned home in the evening alone, instead of having that sinking feeling that harkened back to my feelings as a teenager, after my mother had died and I came home to an empty house, I actually looked forward to the time alone to be with my self! The sadness of loneliness became the pleasure of aloneness.

As I accepted the nurturing feminine side of myself, I began to experience the wise father, my masculine aspect, take firmer hold. I *felt into* the father's strength, creativity, entrepreneurial genius, buoyancy. I called the father to come home.

There was a new order in the household of wayward and lonely selves. The "locals" loved the presence of the matured mother/father and learned to "obey" with pleasure, for it truly felt better to be part of this orderly and loving inner home than wandering lost children crying in the night. Mysteriously, when I honored and matured my inner parents rather than avoiding or escaping from them, they came together as one. When the mother and father are one, there the Essential Self is, and genuine Essential Self governance arises.

As we learn to govern ourselves through inner authority, we become sovereign persons. The vast bureaucracies of prisons, armies, hospitals, police, lawyers, doctors, welfare agents—the entire infrastructure of the world designed to care for, punish, and control local selves—will, I believe, fade away, and the next stage of democracy will subtly take root in those individuals who gain this inner self-governance.

Now, I experience a joined masculine/feminine within me, and I draw on a fused essence of mother/father as a co-creator. They no longer are jousting for control and domination, but rest in true partnership within me. This is the "inner partnership" model. The gender differences have faded into wholeness. I am embodied as a woman, but when I am the Essential Self, I feel so complete that I don't actually notice feminine or masculine differences. The yin and the yang join to form a whole being.

I recorded the transition in my journal:

> This morning I claimed Inner Authority and Self-Governance. I am the Beloved and speak with the authority as the Beloved, with my own local self concerns released and transformed into helpful signals on what needs to be done with no negative charge within me. I can speak from my heart with the authority that is required as my work in the world unfolds.
>
> "Be still and know that I am God" are the words I use to create the alchemical space into which the local selves are now invited by the Teacher Within. It is vital

in here that the local selves respond and adore the Beloved so that they can be absorbed, dis-appear and re-appear as the hands and feet, the eyes and ears, the voice of the Beloved on Earth calling forth to others' essential selves.

When the local selves are in communion with me, experiencing their own absorption into me, I protect them with a radiant shield from the active part that wants to separate to create. Just as worshippers in a church need to be protected in a sacred space from their own daily mundane concerns, so the worshipping local selves need to be protected by me from their mundane concerns. The local selves do not leave the sacred space to go "back" into the so-called real world. They are one with me, and together we go forward as the Universal Human.

Once I claimed authority within myself, the work of inner observation, of dialoguing between the local selves and the Beloved self, became an active, continuous process. My walks in the morning after meditation and journal writing became a time of active inner dialogue. I invited the local self to speak out loud, to say, "I'm really upset about so-and-so." Then Beloved would respond with wisdom and love.

Whatever comes up—having to stand in line at the grocery store, driving in traffic, or getting a call from one of my children who is upset or angry with me—it's all grist for the mill. I no longer get hooked by a problem for long but am able to detach and become a loving authority in dealing with the problem.

Our goal here is not simply to get adjusted or correct a problem within ourselves but to self-evolve into an open-ended, as yet unknown, new human. I have found that the joy of my life now is the unfoldment of myself and others as *that Essential Self which is itself an aspect of infinite, non-dual Reality*, in a continuous process of self-discovery, self-observation, and communion with others doing the same.

In that context, I offer some points of guidance for this stage of development.

The Guidance . . .

We are now ready, as the new integrated identity, the young Universal Human, to accept full authority within ourselves. (The root of the word authority is the Latin *auctor,* meaning creator.) We have been used to exerting external power over others as an egoic self or submitting to some external authority for direction in life. But at this step, we move towards what Gary Zukav, in his book *The Seat of the Soul* (1990), calls "authentic power," by which he means a power which flows from the Essential Self and leads to power from within—true empowerment of self and others.

At this step, the process of emergence is comparable to the path of an astronaut—Jean Houston calls us *psychenauts.* To be selected as an astronaut, one has to display qualities of excellence in all domains—temperament, intelligence, health, and relationships.

A person may get away with sloppiness walking around on the ground, but even one error in outer space can lead to disaster, as happened when the Challenger space shuttle went down due to a defective O-ring. NASA aimed at zero defects and for good reason. Nature is forgiving on Earth, but to reach into outer space, the demands are far more stringent.

The same demands hold true of our emergence as Universal Humans at this stage of our process. But unlike the astronauts, we have no external Mission Control, no external authority we can follow and depend upon. We have only the control or guidance from within ourselves, one which has been enriched with the great teachings of the masters.

We may also draw upon the collective experience of a community of peers undergoing the same process as ourselves, but at the heart of it, we are our own mission control and so must establish a deep inner authority at the level of our Essential Self.

In order for the transfer of power to take place, both essential and local selves must accept a deeper level of responsibility and discipline than ever before. The Essential Self needs to be present and responsible, and the local selves need to give up any remaining desire to act as separated selves. Without this, local selves will infuse the body/mind with their anxiety and prevent the Essential Self from operating.

This is yet another step in the process of the descent of the Beloved and ascent of the local self to join as one, coming into expression as the Universal Human.

Local self must come to believe in the Essential Self's reality and must trust that self to *be* the source of all it seeks in the world. Almaas points out in *Essence* (1986) that ego won't let go until it is assured that everything is in place when he writes:

> "Personality is not going to clear the space completely before it is sure that everything is covered. On the surface it appears that personality wants to displace essence. This is partially true, but on the deeper levels, it was formed and developed ultimately for protection. As essence is discovered, it is easier to let the personality go."

To go the whole way in the Emergence Process, the Essential Self within each of us must gain the trust of the local selves by agreeing to take full responsibility for their behavior and attitudes. This is not power over, but power from within.

As the Essential Self gains authority within the household, it learns to give loving, firm guidance and takes full dominion. The local selves begin to look up to Essential Self for guidance, like children look to the mother when they are confused or angry. Why would they want to follow anyone but her? She has the wisdom, she has the guidance, she offers the love that passeth all understanding.

As the Essential Self assumes operational authority within the household of local selves, we are naturally led to mature our own inner parents, the often undeveloped masculine and feminine aspects of ourselves. The local selves look to the Beloved to have the qualities that ideally our real parents might have had but rarely did.

So many of us came from families that were dysfunctional, headed by parents who did not have a clue about their own or their children's self-development. Now, with the transfer of authority, we are becoming parents to ourselves at a deeper level, actually self-parenting ourselves from within. We must learn to do this job maturely, or there will be rebellion in the inner family, and the local selves will refuse to obey.

In this process of mature self-parenting, addictions and unresolved habitual patterns will come up and must be dealt with. These patterns are often deep and require power and understanding on the part of the Inner Authority to release them from their self-destructive behavior (as well as help from professional therapists where necessary).

Take a Moral Inventory

This time, with the Beloved in authority, take another moral inventory of the issues held by the many local selves. Create a search light and scan through your mindbody for areas of pain, dis-ease, stress, sorrow, fear. As each appears, be utterly compassionate and non-judgmental, as you would toward a wounded child. Choose one of the problem areas and radiate unconditional love to the local self. Invite it into the Rose Chamber to re-experience the Bliss of Union. If that bliss can be genuinely felt by the local self, it will release its patterns far more easily than if it is criticized or overly analyzed.

Once you have brought the wounded self into the bliss of union, *then* and only then, let it speak to you of its experience, holding nothing back. Due to the alchemical process of union, the local self is far more accessible to the guidance of the Beloved and is literally softened and in love.

As the local self speaks to you, the Beloved, draw upon your own intuitive Inner Authority, the creator within. This being knows everything that local selves need to know. The creator within is able to heal, illuminate, and guide your whole being. I have never seen it fail if I do this process. However, it takes time. Local self patterns are amazingly persistent. Keep working in this way, and they will fade away, because, as I have said, they do not want to be in pain and separation any longer, once they have tasted the bliss of union.

As you go through your day, notice every internal signal of pain or stress. Stop. Do not let it flood your nervous system. Bring it up immediately to the loving presence of the Inner Authority.

Assess Your Attitude toward Authority

Examine your attitude toward authority in your life. Have you resented it in others? Have you exerted it over others? Do you approve of the way you handle authority now? Is your sense of internal authority weak or firm? Review your attitude toward your mother and father, and imagine them matured as you would like them to be. Then internalize that parental image as your own. Be the matured parents you didn't have and begin to self-parent your wounded children.

Test the Wisdom of Your Inner Authority

Identify some aspect of your egoic personality that acts up and causes you pain. Invite that local self to the inner court of the Inner Authority. Initiate an inner dialogue and let the local egoic self speak. What is its problem? What is the deeper root of its troubles? Is there a greater meaning to its behavior? Is it trying to do something good? Or is it really self-destructive?

Assess the situation and see if you can draw forth from yourself the wisdom to guide the local self from its patterns of pain. Remember, essence is a direct expression of supreme reality. Its wisdom is unbounded. When you are in resonance with the universal creativity, your essence is all-knowing. Test this out. If you can experience an actual inner healing of a distressing pattern, you gain ever-greater confidence in your capacity as the Inner Authority.

Journal

Be the Inner Authority

Describe a situation in which the local self is acting out an unfulfilling behavior pattern. Develop a poised and still mind. Allow the Inner Authority to come forward and conduct a dialogue with the local self. Have compassion upon the local selves' predicaments. They are suffering the pain of the illusion of separation from you! Nurture them. Work toward an inner family reunion of all the selves. Keep track of successes. Reread your journal. We are learning to be a leader within the household of selves. This is a required ability as we head out to evolve ourselves and the world.

Step Eight: Educating the Local Selves

True Essential Self education begins when we are no longer looking outward to external principalities and powers but are experiencing the Bliss of Union, the Shift of Identity, and the Transfer of Authority as an ongoing, ever-deepening process. It continues as we are willing to learn response-ability for our own emergence and fulfillment as Universal Humans. We are no longer victims. There is no one to blame. We become co-creators of our own reality, entering an inspired dance between the local selves, the Essential Self, other people, and the larger Reality which is informing us all. The choreographer of this divine dance is the universal designing intelligence incarnating in and as us through the Emergence Process.

The Story . . .

I have been involved in the process of emergence for a little over a year now. It has taken patience, self-compassion, and a continual return to bliss. I am amazed at the personal rewards I am receiving. After thirty-five years of inner work, in one year of this process, I am finally free of chronic anxiety, compulsion, and fear of failure. I have learned to reside at the still, quiet center of my being and experience the presence of the Beloved as myself most of the time.

The work I've been doing in the world has taken hold in a new way. It is this process of emergence, still unfolding within me, which I want to offer to all who so desire.

Every morning when I awaken, instead of feeling the twang of nervousness, the sense of being late or behind, I quickly go into the Sunlit Garden of Co-Creation. Because I am not yet fully stabilized, my local selves may be bombarding me with questions and demands, each one pulling me, the Beloved, momentarily out of the Garden. I, Beloved, am still challenged to assume full authority within the household of my selves.

I do not yet have the full radiant power to actually calm the local selves when they are attempting to solve problems in separation from *me*. I have not yet achieved a sustainable, steady state of universal consciousness. Because I do not yet self-remember with continuity of consciousness, my local selves are not sufficiently magnetized to stay in the Sunlit Garden. The "pearl beyond price"— that unique essence I am as the Universal Human—is still developing.

However, the instant I am aware of a separating, judgmental thought arising, I quickly lift the local, grieving self into the Sunlit Garden. If she is deeply distressed, I take her into the Rose Chamber of Union, where she fuses with the divine. Then we move outward into the Sunlit Garden, from the rose to the gold. There, the local self remembers her heart's desire is met. She is content and at home. When ego and essence fuse, regeneration begins. As the stress of separation disappears, the bliss of union spreads. The pleasure centers in the brain flood the system with happiness.

Each day unfolds like an organism progressing toward the unknown. As my local selves are educated, they become willing instruments of my unfoldment—my eyes and ears, my hands and feet in the world. My local selves continue to act up and out, but now that more is happening in my work in the world, I am entering the Sunlit Garden and developing the practice of creating "heaven" in myself.

In the last year, I have actually been freed from every one of those gut-level pains that were part of my driven separate self. I do an emotional internal scan to see if there's any pain left, and if there is, I stop and apply the Almaas technique.

For example, I often feel a chronic impatience with the pace of my work. Irritation and frustration used to flood my nervous system on a daily basis, no matter how hard I worked. Now, instead of letting it override and run me, or trying to ignore or deny it, I penetrate the depth of the feeling. It's a feeling of urgency—"I'll never finish my work!" Or even worse, "The world is running out of time. We won't make it."

Probing the impatience uncovers a hornet's nest—it seems to have legs and arms and a long tail! I penetrate all the way down to the depths, where the self has first felt its separation from God. There, I find the root of this illusory separation, the hopeless feeling that I, egoic self, have to make the world transform. I stop, and because I have been practicing in the Rose Chamber, surrender into the bliss of union. I consciously lift the impatience up into the field of bliss. There, the world is already transformed, and I, the Beloved, am already "there." The goal of my chronic impatience, to do the job of creating a new world, was in truth already fulfilled, right now, by the fact that I am Here!

I wrote in my journal:

> In this Sunlit Garden, I, Beloved, establish this blessed school where the young Universal Human that I am learns to grow. In this sunny Sanctuary I bring up unto me all disconnected local selves trying inadequately to handle problems. I say to all of them, "Come up unto me. I will take your burdens, I will heal your pain. *Stop* trying to figure anything out, or how to solve anything.
>
> Nothing you attempt from your separated state will work. You are *off duty now!* You are to come up higher, past all your local self-contractions, into the field of

lightness, joy, wisdom, and empowerment through resonance with Me, through attunement with the larger design and the actual truth of each situation."

I, Beloved, who has in the past been abstract and discarnate, must truly exercise my presence and authority to create the heaven within where the local selves can meet with me in absolute safety.

In this divine arena of integration and infusion, I exercise for the first time my full authority, love, and wisdom within this household.

In the process of the incarnation of deity, I gain the actual experience of being Lord of this being, not as master, but as "friend." It is the arena in which I, Essential Self, experience myself as fully capable of protecting, nurturing, and guiding this being as a whole person.

It is my place of learning to be fully incarnated, holding the love and intention of all aspects of my self, as a teacher does with disciples.

My local selves are my disciples. I am the teacher within. Now it is my turn to learn to teach, to presence myself with such radiance and attraction that all my local selves are magnetized toward me.

This is the way I create heaven on Earth.

The Guidance . . .

In order to accomplish the education of the local selves, we consciously create an inner space, an expanded Inner Sanctuary where the earlier bliss of union now leads to the incorporation of all local selves into the Beloved. We can visualize this space as the Sunlit Garden of Co-Creation, a place in consciousness of joy, safety, beauty, and love, where the separated selves rejoin the divine and become educated in the power of co-creation—a personal kindergarten for godlings.

Here is the alchemical cauldron where the transformation of the person takes place. Here, we become fully human and fully divine, that is, a Universal Human.

In this Garden, the Beloved resides permanently. It is her domain and she rules with unconditional love, sitting upon her seat of authority in the kingdom of heaven within. She invites the household of local selves to enter, calling them to freedom from the pain of separation, from the addiction to their strategies that are not working any longer.

The local selves flock to her eagerly, freely and voluntarily giving up their pursuit of happiness in separation. They gather at her feet to gaze upward toward her with the same adoration that disciples have for their gurus. She is their guru, their "advantage." In her presence, they are released from bondage to their pain of separation, to their unfulfilled ambitions, their sense of failure, and lack of self-worth. She is fulfilling their heart's desire. A magnetic attraction pulls the disciples toward her. They are willing to commit to the self-discipline required for full integration with her.

Just as devotees empower the guru, the adoring local selves energize the Essential Self. We experience new empowered capacities—self-presencing, self-radiating, self-impressing—which deepen and strengthen as the local selves focus attention on the Beloved, enabling her to come into full force within us.

In this vibrational field of devotion, the egoic selves are fully relaxed and attentive. They want to be with the Beloved, indeed, to be consummated through union with her much like the mystic's passion for union with God. Only this passion turns inward toward the God-self, the unique and personal essence of the divine *as* each of us.

The teacher in Garden is the Beloved within each of us, informed by the accumulated wisdom of the sacred traditions, the literature, the arts and sciences of humanity. In the earlier developmental path, we looked outside our-selves to the great masters of the world's religious and spir-itual traditions or their current representatives. But on this new path, we have direct access to the master teacher within ourselves.

Kindergarten begins for each young Universal Human when the teacher within shows up and begins to exercise wisdom and guidance for all the local selves, who in the past have been trying to run the world and failed. Now, true guid-ance and authority comes from within each student, each emerging human, and from within the emerging community.

To educate our local selves, we must deal with their various aspects: the good local self, the anxious, the dis-tressed local selves. We also must deal with the deeper problem from which all local selves spring, the illusion of our separation from God and each other. We focus on prac-tices which train our local selves and lead to our full emer-gence as Universal Humans.

The milieu in which this education best takes place is an expanded state of bliss, a true culture of ecstasy. The local selves absorb the vibrational field of the Beloved such that the alchemical process is accelerated within them. In order for this to happen, discipline is required, but not the discipline of rewards and punishment. There is no force or compulsion here. It's the discipline of actually experienc-ing yourself as you are already there, which is ecstatic.

In the Garden, the course of studies offered is everything the local selves could possibly desire: the bliss of union, the promise of the fusion of genius, the explosion of their cre-ativity, the ecstasy of co-creation—the full incarnation as divinity. Joy. Gladness. Heaven on Earth within *us!* Who would turn this down if they knew its fabulous rewards?

One of our first tasks is to practice freeing ourselves from all pressure of time—local self's compulsion to "get the job done" before time runs out. We have dealt with the pressure of time in the Inner Sanctuary, but now we practice under the guidance of our Essential Self as authority.

Here we learn to move from local, linear time (the domain of local self) to non-local, nonlinear time, the pure experience of the present (the domain of Essential Self). In this process, the local selves realize that of themselves they can do nothing. The Father/Mother, the Great Creating Process, "doeth the work." We come to realize that this inner union *is* the job that needs to get done to transform anything in oneself and the world. *This* is the fundamental work which will best serve the world.

Freedom from the urgency of time releases the local selves, allowing them to be absorbed in the vibrational field of the Beloved's ever-present Now. In this field, local self's problems and issues are dissolved, not solved. When we shift our attention down to the level of the problems we are trying to solve, we descend in our vibration. From this vantage point, we feel separate and cannot solve our problems. But once the local selves are lifted up into the love field of the Beloved, their stress is released, their patterns are dissolved, and in that divine milieu Beloved can point out the truth of the situation to the local selves.

In this process, we learn to create a new center of gravity in ourselves. Instead of our local self's thoughts and concerns drawing Beloved's attention downward, contaminating the nervous system with stress, we create a new and stronger thought field of attraction. This field magnetizes wayward thoughts before they impact the nervous system. If we can learn to take a negative thought up quickly, before it enters our nervous system, we will not be affected by the thought. This is self-evolution through self-elevation.

However, if certain patterns of worry, blame, or impatience persist, seeming to resist being repatterned in the field, we may need to deal with them more directly. I have found the technique described by Almaas in his "Diamond

Approach" helpful and have adopted it in my inner work when a local self issue chronically reoccurs, even after being lifted up.

Almaas (*Essence*, 1986) suggests we directly experience the deficiencies of the ego or local self and recognize that what the ego is attempting to get is already present in Essence. The process here is to feel deeply ego's lack, or "hole" as Almaas calls it, and not defend against this feeling of lack, nor come up with any strategies for solving the problem from the egoic point of view.

It is a two-step process: First, the Beloved invites the local selves to come forward to describe as deeply as possible any pain or deficiency being experienced—the needs, wants, pain. We don't defend against the feeling, don't try to fix or solve it from the egoic point of view, but rather completely allow it to be present and fully feel it—its location in the body, its density, vibration. Second, we stay with that pain and follow it all the way to the root, the source where we first felt such pain.

According to Almaas, when we follow the deficiency as deeply as possible, it leads us to that part of essence or Beloved that the local self has been seeking by trying to have some strategy in the outer world. In other words, we let our local selves discover that the fulfillment they've been seeking is already present in the Beloved. Ego becomes the guide to essence.

Almaas describes the process in *Essence*:

> When one allows oneself quietly to experience the hurtful wound and memories connected with it, the golden elixir will flow out of it, healing it, and filling the emptiness with the beautiful sweet fullness that will melt the heart, erase the mind, and bring about the contentment that the individual has been thirsting for. . . . Ego's search for satisfaction being over, because you're

not defending, not strategizing, leads you to that part of
the Pearl that it's been seeking by strategizing.

The miracle is that the ego self feels suddenly fulfilled,
like finding within its own essence what it's been seeking
in the world.

We discover that underneath all specific symptoms
which feel so personal and unique, there is usually one fundamental
source from which the particular problem
springs. That is ego's separation from essence, or in traditional
language, the human separation from God.
Therefore, the prime solution to almost all our problems is
the reunion of ego and essence. This is the shortcut to
human transformation.

When the problem is brought up into the domain of the
Essential Self, with probing intelligence the Essential Self
helps the local self see that the source of the problem is its
own illusion of separation. It reveals that the Beloved within
holds the very qualities local self was seeking outside.

In the field of resonance, the ego experiences a
reunion with essence and the pain disappears. The local
self releases its sense of judgment on itself and others. It
stops trying to negotiate and be right and experiences compassion
for itself and others, taking on the vantage of the
Beloved toward itself. *The local selves become wise enough
to see themselves through the eyes of their own divinity.* From
this view, there is no right and wrong, no good and no evil,
only truth, and the truth sets us free of judgment.

In the resonant field, local self distress is unstressed.
Egoic problems are not in the first instant solved. They are
dissolved. In the resonant vibrational field of the divine
essence, problems fade and no longer seem to exist.

As our local selves are educated, they begin to become
the instruments of our unfoldment. They are our eyes and
ears, our hands and feet in the world.

At this step in our Emergence Process, genuine compassion for others occurs. Those who are suffering from hunger, poverty, war, and illness cannot, unless they are heroic, practice their own emergence. It is up to us who have the freedom to practice to do so and then to reach out to others less fortunate than ourselves, both to heal and eventually to serve as guides upon the path of self-evolution, each in our own way. For ultimately, the root cause of hunger, poverty, violence, and greed is the separation of our egos from the one Essential Self that each of us is.

Create an Inner Sunlit Garden of Co-Creation

You can create this space early in the morning, even for half an hour as you lie in bed half-awake. Invite your local selves to be with you in complete seclusion, where they have absolutely nothing to do and nowhere to go. Let them experience the truth that everything they have sought is already given to them through their union with the Beloved, always, already present. Let the local selves have this blessed, uninterrupted time with the Beloved in safety and bliss.

You will find that throughout the day the Garden resides at the core of your being. Mundane events are infused with the presence of the Beloved. You realize that life itself is being transformed by you. You become more clearly the cause of your own experience rather than at the effect of it. You are a co-creator.

Let Ego Guide You to Essence

Practice the Almaas technique by focusing on your "holes," or deficiencies, presented to you by the local self. Select some aspect of your being that feels pain or is grieving, lacking in something. In the Sunlit Garden, take time to focus on the deficiency. Feel it as deeply as possible for as long as needed. Be completely open, with no thoughts of how to "fix it" or make it better.

Just let it *be* fully, whatever it is, with no resistance whatsoever. Then wait, as Almaas suggests, for ego to guide you precisely to the quality within yourself that you have been seeking. Ego becomes your guide to Essence. Then, contemplate, cultivate, love that quality in your Essential Self that ego has been fruitlessly seeking. Be present as that quality. Let it sink in. In this way, you "metabolize" your ego. Ego is consumed in the alchemical furnace of essence, the great transformer within.

Use your Inner Authority to set up the conditions for ego to bring forth the very qualities of essence that you seek. Even one success in this process will encourage you to do more. For example, when I let the grieving girl guide me to the mother she had sought, I was then convinced that I can heal any aspect of my personality that I can discover. The Essential Self always knows the next step needed for our own healing. We can rest assured that the teacher within truly knows everything we need to know.

Call upon the Great Ones

Most of us at this stage of the "new normalcy" are, at best, Junior Beloveds. Be humble. We are all at the beginning of our emergence as Universal Humans. Call upon your spiritual guides and teachers, whoever inspires you, living or dead, to be guides as Senior Beloveds. In their field, we can stabilize, not as devotees, but as younger sisters and brothers, replicating their essence as a new norm in the world.

Consciously Call the Mature Inner Parents
to Deal with Every Local Self Issue

Feel within yourself the matured mother and father as the Inner Authority. That is your power now. Have no fear of exerting that power fully within yourself, for its purpose is the empowerment of your whole being. When a local self is in pain or distress, take it up to you—do not descend down to its level. Let it feel the bliss of union with you and remind it that its fundamental problem is separation from you. If there is any residue of problem left, have a dialogue between the local and Beloved self to get at the truth of the matter. Remember, the Beloved teacher within knows everything your local self needs for its healing and whole-ing.

Acknowledge the Good in
Most Local Self Motivation

Underneath the stress of local self's efforts to succeed, to win self esteem, to prevail in the world, is a deeper motivation that is found to reside in the Essential Self. That motivation is often good but misguided. Ego is working for your safety and success in the world. Once it is incorporated into the Beloved, the ego reappears as the executive capacities of your whole being to bring your essence into form in the world. Thank the local selves for their devotion to their purpose of protecting you. Once the Beloved is actually in charge, the good motivation of local selves has been fulfilled. They are ready to release their illusions and compulsions.

Do unto Others' Local Selves
What You Can Do for Your Own

To the degree that we can guide our own local selves, we can be compassionate and helpful to another's egoic personality. When we learn not to judge our own egoic personality, we are far less judgmental to others. As we learn to presence ourselves as the Beloved, we can transmit the Beloved to the Beloved in others. This transmission awakens the inner presence in other people, and they begin to access their own inner Essential Self. They are lifted up by your presence.

Firmly Close the Door

It may be true that local selves no longer want to escape into addictive patterns, yet the patterns of separation are extremely deep and persistent. It helps here, once again, to close the door with a definitive internal gesture of finality. Here are some suggested affirmations, and feel free to write your own.

This is the end of separation. I have crossed the great divide. I will not go back again. I may be young, but I am born. I will never return to the illusion of separation.

This set of clear affirmations trains local selves not to revert to old patterns of escape and ego-driven compulsions.

Be Alert to the Recurrence of Chronic Anxiety

Develop a sensitive biofeedback system to alert you to anxiety. The instant you feel anxiety, stop and do not let it override you. Anxiety simply means the local self has taken charge in the household of selves. The Beloved, now the Inner Authority, needs to respond quickly, just like a parent would to a child who is about to fall down and hurt itself. The moment you feel anxiety, stop. Breath yourself quickly into the environment of the Rose Chamber. If you have practiced in the morning, it will be easily accessed when needed. (Or use whatever technique works for you to return to center. The Emergence Process has as many ways as there are individuals. Invent your own.)

Read the Outline of the Entry Course:
Gateway to Our Conscious Evolution (page 155)
And enroll on the Internet.

Choose to Read Some of the Seminal Books Offered in the Conscious Evolution Library (page 173)

As you read, ask yourself what this work means for your own emergence. Expand your Emergence Circle into your own evolutionary study group.

Journal

Organize Your Journal

I recommend that you create several sections in your journal. In one section, abstract and keep a record of the Beloved's voice. Another section would be "problems in progress," where you describe a grievance, pain, anxiety, and work it through. Don't expect that this will be handled in one session with the Beloved—that's unrealistic. If it's a very deep problem, it will take some time for most of us, certainly for me—although sometimes something amazing happens, such as a sudden remission from a toxic emotion.

Practice the Almaas technique by sitting with that deficiency until it leads you to the quality of Essence that ego is seeking outside. Write that down. If the problem comes up again, bring it into the Rose Chamber. Does Beloved have something important to say? Write that down. Keep an inventory of your progress in dealing with things that are persistently difficult for you. You will know you have graduated when those problems disappear.

Meditation

Read this meditation. Listen to Emergence Meditation tapes (to be ordered from the Foundation for Conscious Evolution).

Locate within your heart a point of pure white light,
the open space within you where spirit pours forth its

radiance, animating and informing your essence. It is the place where universal creativity infuses your personal essence with the radiant presence of the divine. Feel the entire process of creation that animates all being focusing in your heart as your own impulse of emergence.

Place your consciousness in this center. It is your direct contact with Source. Let this universal presence infuse your personal essence with the white light. Your Beloved self is now fusing with Source. You are one with the universal mind of God. Then expand gently outward into the Rose Chamber of Union of the Human and the Divine. Place your identity in the Beloved, feeling its radiance and warmth.

Invite all your local selves to enter into union with you. Let the weary and wounded egoic selves float into the Rose Colored Chamber. Radiate your divine vibration upon them. Dissolve their density. Release their contractions. Entrain them in your vibrational field until they are consumed in your radiance, and vibrate at the frequency of the Beloved. Feel all your local selves fuse with YOU.

Experience the bliss of union.

Now open the delicate membrane of the Rose Chamber into the Sunlit Garden of *Co-Creation*, where other young Universal Humans play. Let the energized local selves enter the garden. It is the second inner sanctuary. It is filled with flowers, scents, sights, tastes, sounds, and beauty that delight and charm the local selves. It is a place of play, a kindergarten of godlings.

Visualize masters of the past and present looking on benignly, supervising at a distance. Bring forth your most beloved spiritual teachers and ancestors. Allow them to be with you, to bless and embrace you in joy at your appearance among them. They have been waiting for your arrival for a long time. Let them infuse you with their essence and qualities of being you most desire. Ask that those qualities be incarnate in you. Feel each of them. Affirm their presence as you.

Consummate your union with the divine beings who have gone before and are paving the way for your emergence. Luxuriate and play in the Inner School for Conscious Evolution.

Step Nine:
The Repatterning of Life

At this final step in our Childhood, we ripen and come to a new level of maturity in our development as Universal Humans. Just as a child attending school for the first time is awkward and then gradually gains confidence, so are we, as young Universal Humans, gradually coming into a greater Essential Self confidence, a deeper trust of our inner knowing, a new way of relating to one another. We are at home in the kindergarten of the godlings.

At this step, the more we let go of egoic fears, the more we find that our external life reflects the deeper guidance and motivation of the Essential Self. There is a coincidental relationship between inner integration and outer manifestation. We see clear demonstration that the inner creates the outer, that intention manifests, that our consciousness is causal in the events, relationships, projects, and visions of our lives.

The Story . . .

As the Emergence Process accelerated within me, I found myself trying to hold onto my old pattern out of fear that I would be left bereft. I clung to my familiar life pattern, *knowing* that it was not working as it was, especially in my work and my relationship. But I was afraid to let go.

Despite my fearful efforts to maintain it, the old pattern disintegrated and fell away. I went through a period of panic. Chaos seemed to be everywhere. It felt like "failure," but in retrospect I see that, as is so often the case, the breakdown was absolutely essential to allow the breakthrough to occur.

A few months before this period, while giving a talk for the *Mind/SuperMind* lecture series offered in Santa Barbara, California, I had asked my audience a rhetorical, spontaneous question at the end of my presentation: "What would happen if this whole community were to experience its own potential for conscious evolution?"

That very night, 185 people signed up to discover the answer. A seed group formed and began a plan to bring me to Santa Barbara to teach a class. I would use the Curriculum I had been working on in Marin County as the basis for bringing forth Conscious Evolution in an entire community. (This curriculum has evolved into the Entry Course: Gateway to Our Conscious Evolution. See page 155 for an outline.)

In the interim, when I visited Santa Barbara frequently to work with the seed group, I felt a remarkable resonance. Each person seemed to be emerging in his or her own way. I shared the ideas about the coming of the Universal Human. A resonant field received me. My own experience was echoing back throughout the experience of others. I fell in love with everyone.

When I returned in May of 1999 to do the teaching, my beloved colleague, friend, and now co-director of the Foundation for Conscious Evolution, Teresa Collins, said to me, "Barbara, this the first time you will be able to tell the story as a whole."

She was right. I could do it, because on the one hand, I was emerging as the Essential Self. On the other hand, I was speaking into the listening of people who were responding to the same impulse within themselves. I was not telling "about" the story; I was speaking as an expression of the story myself. Most important, this was not a conference or an event; it was a gathering of pioneering souls who happened to live in one place.

I asked them whether they would work together for a year or two to explore the new path of self and social evolution together. The response was overwhelmingly positive, and the first conscious evolutionary community formed.

Meanwhile, the operations of the Foundation for Conscious Evolution in northern California collapsed. People I loved and was loyal to, whom I would never have let go, got sick and had to stop. My office was moved by members of the new team. A house and office were found, furnished, and prepared while I was away at a teaching event. Talented co-creators stepped forward for various tasks! Co-creative community was forming spontaneously.

Within the last year, from 1999 to 2000, my external life has re-patterned itself. Evolution usually works in small incremental steps, but occasionally it takes quantum leaps into discontinuous, radical newness. In macrocosmic evolution, this is called "punctuated equilibrium." Sudden jumps also occur in our microcosmic lives, activated by years of subtle events which cannot be understood until the jump occurs. Then it can be seen from the other side of the leap that everything that happened needed to happen.

Now I look back from the other side of my leap—a year and a half since I entered the Inner Sanctuary in Marin County—sitting in my little studio in Santa Barbara, looking out upon a small rose garden, writing *Emergence* as a young Universal Human to reach out to other kindred souls. Everything I have conceived over the last thirty-five years is now coming into form.

When I have shared this story with other evolutionary leaders, I find that they are experiencing the same phenomenon. If we persevere in our inner growth and in our vocational callings, in humility, faith, and good cheer, the process itself will often jump our life and work ahead into a new domain that fulfills our deepest heart's desire.

I have learned that it is vital in the early days of our emergence to follow that "compass of joy" through the darkness of our confusion. It will lead to fulfillment if we will only stay the course. As Churchill said during the Second World War, "Never give in, never, never, never . . . except to conditions of honor and good sense."

I have found that my heart's deepest desire for more life, for higher consciousness and greater freedom, has never guided me falsely. I give thanks that I have followed that profound passion that led me from my agnostic background, to my years of wife and mother, to my early years as a visionary futurist, to this threshold at the dawn of my seventh decade, at a new beginning. *Follow your bliss,* as Joseph Campbell tells us. It is the light to guide us through the night into the brilliant Sunlit Garden of Co-Creation where the continuous future begins.

The daily journal writing intensified as "I" the Beloved consciously wrote as the I AM to my local selves:

I am calling you to the complete family reunion within Me. Bring the separated mind home to the God within. Through this fusion of selves within we will come through the fire of alchemical transformation from our creature to our co-creative phase.

Have no fear in Santa Barbara. It is our teaching of this that will bring in everything we need as we need it.

Place all your burdens in Me. We will "allow the Tao" to carry us through the river of universal creativity to our appropriate destination within the design of creation. Our will joins universal design of creation—wholes within wholes within wholes.

You, local selves, release your anxiety and allow Me, who is one with the Great Creating Process, to lift you up unto the radiant, self-transcending process of creation out of which we are continuously being created. This double fusion, local self with Essential Self, and Essential Self with cosmic universal Source, is the key to full-scale co-creation of new worlds. It is the process of the evolution of the person from *Homo sapiens* to *Homo universalis*.

You, local selves, in all your diversity and individuality, now release your burdens completely and enter the Holy of Holies, the Rose Chamber of Union of the Human and the Divine. Here you must dwell in blissful union every day during this vital period of repatterning. Otherwise, the alchemical process is aborted, the old anxieties flood your system, and you are set back further than if you never began. This is a dangerous period.

The Guidance . . .

As we shift our attention and identity to the Essential Self and experience the world outside from this inner vantage point, the outer action seems miraculously to repattern itself to a higher order, one that is more resonant with our inner values. The steps we are to take in accomplishing our work are revealed spontaneously.

Ease of effort replaces overwhelm. Peace dissolves anxiety, panic, and nervousness. The external process flows from within and reflects the power and authority of the Essential Self. "As above, so below."

When we take our attention off our strategies to get things done, when ego steps aside and essence is in dominion, life becomes a process of creative discovery. Internal compulsion relaxes its grip. We begin to flow in our work spontaneously and to unfold organically with others.

At first, however, this external repatterning of our lives can be difficult, not what we may have expected. Dysfunctionalities, situations that have not worked for years, aspects of our lives that are out of alignment with our Essential Self, begin to show up. They become intolerable in contrast with the new inner harmony.

The dissonance at this more advanced stage can actually abort the alchemical process and be more destructive than dissonance was when we were more fully egoic. The contrast is sharper and thus more painful, making it seem as though everything is breaking down. But it is vital to the process that this breakdown be allowed to proceed without fear.

If we can stay centered, relax, and "let go, let God," as the popular saying goes, we will find that dysfunctionalities begin to drop away, while on the other hand, new "functionalities" appear. Things that seemed impossible to manifest before now begin to happen effortlessly. "Miracles" happen but they are only miracles from the perspective of the separated mind. From the point of view of the attuned Beloved, they are natural. At this stage, the willingness to tolerate ambiguity and uncertainty is a prize quality for our continued emergence.

When new order starts forming out of chaos in our own lives, we realize we too are part of the self-organizing universe that brought us from subatomic particles to this very instant of time. It is no more miraculous that we should evolve into a higher order than that subatomic particles made atoms and that molecules made cells.

Everything is miraculous and mysterious beyond the understanding of the rational mind. Yet we *are* that very nature which we are attempting to understand from the outside.

As we release our bondage to the separated self, we enter more deeply the organic unfoldment of nature, that is, human nature. We are in alignment with the deeper patterns that are creating all existence and us. After all, nature arose and is continuously arising out of an invisible, nonphysical field able to self-organize from *no thing* at all to *everything that is,* following a deep tendency toward higher consciousness and greater freedom through more complex order. We are expressions of that transcendent, awesome, magnificent, universal organizing intelligence.

When our separated minds quiet down, our deeper self, which is one with that intelligence, comes forth. This emergence is the purpose of meditation, and it is also the process of incarnation and co-creation. We learn to sustain the internal resonance of our inner state as we work in the world. We learn to maintain resonance with others, doing the work together. In fact, *being* and *doing* blend together seamlessly.

We see this in nature. We do not look at a leaf and ask, "Is it *being* or *doing*?" It is simply being itself—*leafing.* When we are at one with the essence of our being, we lose "self" consciousness. We are in the flow; we are the very essence expressing itself.

If subatomic particles could make atoms, and atoms could make molecules, and molecules cells, and so on up the great spiral of evolution, then surely we can Essential Self-organize to fulfill our own creative potential in cooperation with others doing the same. It is natural. What is *unnatural* is the illusion that we are separate from that cosmic intelligence that is creating everything that is.

Ken Wilber writes in *One Taste* (1999) how our essence expresses in the process of creation:

> Once you find your formless identity as Buddha-mind, as Atman, as pure Spirit or Godhead, you will take that constant, non-dual, ever-present consciousness and reenter the lesser states . . . reanimate them with radiance. . . . You will pour yourself out into the mind and

world, and create them in the process, and enter them all equally, but especially and particularly that specific mind and body that is called you. . . . You will then awaken as radical freedom, and sing those songs of radiant release, beam an infinity too obvious to see, and drink an ocean of delight. . . .

To stabilize yourself in day-to-day life as a young Universal Human requires deep perseverance, radical faith, and the profoundly loving devotion of a parent for a child who wakes crying in the middle of the night. We need to nurture our own Emergence Process, because as the Beloved we are parenting and training the still vulnerable and wayward local selves.

The following are some practices to support this process and some attitudes to adopt and cultivate as you mature in this phase of Childhood, beginning the transition into the Youth of the Universal Human.

Allow Your Life to Repattern

Shift from controlling your daily life through planning and organizing to include elements of discovery, appreciation, and resonance in all your activities. By letting go of control, you allow a new pattern to unfold. Be receptive to synergies, synchronicities, suprasexual attractions as they appear in your projects and relationships. Allow space for the visionary aspect of the Beloved to infuse you with inspiration. Cultivate the feeling of joy.

Self-Presencing

The best practice at this stage is to center yourself in the Beloved and remain calm at the core of the chaos, placing your intention into the field and allowing the organizing process to reveal the way. Practice feeling the essence of the Beloved as yourself, peaceful, all-knowing, fulfilled, always already present as the Presence. Remember that You are the Beloved. The Beloved knows and has guided you until this moment. Now you are that guide. You are *it*. Our faith makes us whole.

Radiate the Presence

There is always entropy—the tendency in closed systems toward increased disorder—and syntropy, or negentropy—the fifteen-billion-year tendency to form a higher, more complex order—operating in our lives. The entropic disorder is the very raw material out of which the new order, that is, our repatterned lives, to a higher order occurs.

To guide your internal system from succumbing to fear and inertia (entropy) and to move toward love, life purpose, and co-creativity (syntropy), radiate the presence of the Essential Self, lifting the arising fears and resistance to change up unto the higher frequencies of the Essential Self where they are repatterned. These dense patterns of self-contraction are gradually erased by radiance and deep relaxation.

Realize That You Are Fully Response-Able

You can respond to every need that is coming before you. Affirm that, as the Beloved, you are not needy, afraid, or lonely. You are attracting every resource and person you need. You are entering the finest time of your life. You are ready to come into new form, informed by the process of creation itself.

Cultivate Resonance by Attuning with Others

In this early phase of repatterning, it is vital to draw to you two or more to create a field of resonance, a growth culture for the young Universal Human. The repatterning of our lives leads to co-creation, but it takes time. The formation of small resonant circles—the two or more gathered—is vital at this stage. Do not try to do this alone. You need the "field." It is like mother's milk to the newly born Universal Human.

Nourish the Beloved

Create a special place in your meditation to simply *be* your Essential Self, without paying any attention to the needs and demands of local selves. We do not want to have a work-a-day Beloved, getting worn out by attending to needs of the local selves, like a mother with a colicky child. Take time for the Beloved to plug into the radiant, non-dual, infinite reality and dwell in its real home which is God. Only then will the beautiful "Pearl" have the strength of radiance to deal with its ongoing work of raising and educating the household of local selves. Only thus will the process of incarnation fulfill itself.

Journal

Write a description of what is falling away in your life and what is emerging that is new. Do you see the new patterns of personal breakthrough out of breakdown? Allow your deepest heart's desire for more life, for higher consciousness, and greater freedom to express itself fully. Describe the desire. Intend it. Affirm it. Declare it as already potentially so. Describe the learning from every incident. Practice writing as the Great Creating Process that is You. Realize that the "force of creation" is with you—as you!

Youth

Step Ten: Fulfilling the Promise

We are crossing the threshold from our Childhood into the vast and as yet uncharted realm of our Youth as Universal Humans. We are undergoing a new rite of passage, yet to be acknowledged in this world. To prepare, we first cast our eye backward in time to see the exquisite pattern of our emergence, guided silently and mysteriously by our essential selves.

We remember our conception and gestation, our first awakenings in the womb of self-consciousness, our resonance with spiritual ancestors and guides, our woundings, our vocational arousal, our willingness to say yes to the birth of our emerging selves, our desire to co-create with others. We honor the definitive moment of recognition that our growth is no longer possible when driven by our egoic local self. We are born, sometimes gracefully, other times painfully, and we enter our Infancy where we contemplate the glory of the Beloved within.

Through our attention, we learn to magnetize the incarnation of the deeper self; we invite the Essential Self to take dominion within the household of selves and experience the bliss of union with our divine essence. From there, we enter our Childhood, shifting our identity from ego to essence, transferring authority to the Beloved within, and beginning the life-long process of educating our local selves and repatterning our lives.

At last, we arrive in the developmental path at a very early phase of Youth, ready now to come into form in the evolution of our selves and our world. Like our forerunners in the cultures of the past who separated out youths from the tribe at puberty and initiated them in the ways of adulthood, so we initiate ourselves together in the ways of the evolving human growing in us now. We celebrate within us the shift from the creature human to the co-creator.

The Story . . .

The transition between Childhood and Youth, similar to the transition between Infancy and Childhood, is not marked by a sudden shift but by a gradual unfolding. Yet one day, I woke up and noticed that a very real phase change had taken place, a shift as definitive as that from pre-puberty to puberty, or from menarche to menopause. I felt that I had graduated from Childhood. I now reside as the Essential Self and am ready to commit to action at a larger scale. This is the new hero's journey and all emerging Universal Humans are on it.

As I enter Youth now, I am in the process of securing my identity in essence rather than ego and am taking full responsibility for the household of my many and wayward local selves. It is clear that my life has been repatterned, as the outward manifestation more and more reflects the inner knowing.

As of this writing, in the summer of 2000, the work in Santa Barbara is flourishing. Of course, all of this will change and evolve, so I am hesitant to be overly specific. We discover that we are part of a living social organism. All the work is interconnected. We are connecting with partners, collaborative initiatives, and enterprises throughout the world.

The various teachings are offered as ways for individuals to enter the process of self and social evolution. "The Entry Course: Gateway to Our Conscious Evolution" (See page 154.) is now available. The Santa Barbara community is experimenting with social processes and synergistic structure to enable all its members to give their gifts and will offer tools and templates to any community wishing to do the same. We will draw upon the ever-unfolding Peace Room website, which is scanning for, mapping, and connecting with those now transforming our world (www.peaceroom.org).

The Peace Room is being developed as a resource for students to find their teammates, mentors, and guides in fulfilling their vocational arousal. Through our program on Wisdom Radio on the Internet, *Live from the Peace Room* at 5 P.M. PST (www.wisdommedia.com), we are reaching out across the globe to pioneering souls, joining the larger community, inviting emerging leadership in all fields to use this program to express their own breakthroughs and "new" news, hot off the evolutionary griddle! We realize that we are forming a first "Center for the Conscious Evolution of Humanity" in Santa Barbara.

Everything I have ever thought of is "coming true" in new form. None of it have I done before. I am constantly stretching, challenged to go beyond my past limits, getting newer every day.

Yet, in the midst of all this activity, I have finally come to realize that my "goal" is not any external activity, important as goals are, but rather myself emerged, stabilized, and whole as a new norm, in loving relationship with and in support of others doing the same.

For thirty-five years, I have had a purpose in the world to "go tell the story of the birth of a Universal Humanity."

Although Essential Self had signaled me for years to "create an aura of silence about you until you can hear me at all times . . . until your self-centered mind is fully incorporated in your God-centered mind," local self ignored the focus on the Beloved and continued to feel compelled to work in the world, overriding the deeper guidance for Self realization.

Now, in my Youth, rewarded by the bliss of union, I have finally followed this guidance and am experiencing the "rewards." Deepening and sharing this process of inner union, communion, and co-creating is the primary purpose of my mission on Earth. While it will take generations for the next phase of social evolution to unfold, it is also true that this experience is available within us now and is the wellspring out of which the new world comes.

The shift of identity is quantum; that is, it jumps from one orbit to the next with no distance in between, like an electron. I don't have to get here. I am here. Then, once I am aware of that, I can unfold in time/space. And it is from this position, at the other side of the quantum jump, already here as the Universal Human, that we can best guide ourselves through this period of quantum transformation and radical newness.

As long as I was thinking that I had to fulfill some external goal, I was prevented by that very striving from being the goal I was intending. I realize now that this being-ness is my purpose. For only as this being can I "do" what I am to do.

If I do what I do as one who is trying to reach a goal, driven by my good ego, that goal will forever recede from my grasp, and I will forever be grasping. However, if I am the goal, if the Universal Human incarnate is the goal right now, then I am forever liberated from seeking or grasping at anything, and my work will have a quality that truly serves others as it serves myself.

As Universal Humans, we unfold, expressing ourselves moment by moment in our work in the world. In that unfoldment, whatever we are meant to do, we can trust will happen spontaneously.

This is the first moment in my whole life in which I have ever felt that my purpose is fulfilled. By accepting this state of being as my purpose fulfilled, I have taken a quantum leap.

As Almaas (*Essence*, 1986) says: "A person living in the present can have goals, but the goals are an expression and the result of who the person is at the moment. The person is already fulfilled and that fulfillment can then manifest as certain goals. . . . Goals are compensations for the absence of the Essential Self. . . . "

The Guidance . . .

What are the fruits of this new phase of being? How does it serve others? Being the Essential Self in person is the ultimate service to humanity, because then we transmit that essence to others spontaneously, helping others to shift from ego to essence by our presence.

Hold a Mirror for Others to See Who They Truly Are

We become mirrors in which others can see the "glory" of who they truly are. By holding a clear surface for others to see themselves as we see them, we mature ourselves as Universal Humans as we serve others. And as we make the shift from ego to essence, we can better guide the larger society through its transition from collective egoic behavior, as expressed in vast military spending, nuclear proliferation, environmental destruction, and so on. We cannot transform the world as local selves, no matter how well motivated we are.

Access within Yourself an Expanded Guide,
a More Profound Aspect of the Inner Beloved

Call upon this presence to provide the deeper wisdom you need to bring yourself out into the world into form that expresses your Essential Self.

For example, I found that a new facet of my Essential Self has emerged. I call her my "Cosmic Guide." Her keynote is wisdom. When I am in doubt as to what to do next, I place my attention in the Essential Self and call for the Cosmic Guide, who answers to the name *Sophia*, the goddess of wisdom. When local self clenches and says, "What shall I do?" my Sophia appears. She literally stops the local self thought pattern of anxiety from arising before it hits the threshold of consciousness and replaces it with her signature flash of endorphin-induced relaxation, warmth, trust, and love.

She "knows" what to do, but she won't "tell" until local self releases the anxiety and agrees to bask in her cosmic intelligence which is attuned to the larger patterns of creation. Local self must turn off for her to turn on.

When the Cosmic Guide turns on, local self regains the "poised mind" it has acquired through asking and receiving guidance in meditation and journal writing. Now the journal writing becomes the journey of daily life. The Emergence Process is a moment-by-moment practice of including the Cosmic Guide, of turning all guidance over to her.

This Cosmic Guide is, of course, a vital aspect of Essential Self. She is not called into play until the life conditions outside warrant her wisdom. She does not show up in her commanding radiance in Infancy and Childhood, when the tasks are more rudimentary. Now, in Youth, we are actually moving outward to invent, innovate, and co-create something new.

Surrender the Figuring-It-Out Mind

The guidance for newness comes from the profound pattern of evolutionary design embedded in nature and in human nature. In the presence of our deepening wisdom, we surrender the figuring-it-out mind. We bring to waking consciousness the inner intuitive knowing, the gnosis, as a continual wise presence, now fully incarnated and doing the work through the agency of the local selves. We quiet the "waters of the mind" moment by moment, for life itself is the meditation. The mind remains poised, and the essential love/intelligence emerges in each instant. Life becomes a continual conversion experience.

Have Compassion upon Yourself

We must have compassion upon ourselves. There is no one on this Earth, as far as we know, who has been through a planetary phase change from the high technology, overpopulating, polluting phase to the next phase of universal co-creative evolution, which we are envisioning as our possible future. This macrocosmic "birth transition" is not taught in our great universities. There are no experts in planetary transformation because no one has lived through it.

While there are many spiritual schools for the evolution of the person toward God realization, there are, as we have noted, few places where we learn to be co-creators of the next stage of self and social evolution. Our "Entry Course: Gateway to Our Conscious Evolution" is one of the first efforts to discover what a species does when it is facing the choice of self-induced extinction or conscious evolution for the first time.

As we enter our Youth, we have few models of adults to guide us. In fact, we must become what Sidney Thomas Lanier calls "elders from the future" ourselves. We cast our imaginations and intuitions forward to tap into a deeper knowing of our personal and collective potential and, from that new vantage point in our own imagined and chosen futures, guide ourselves through the "puberty" phase of our early youth as Universal Humans.

Become the "Future Present"

As we learn to mature the inner parents to act as our guiding authority, so now we mature ourselves in our future-oriented knowing. We allow our deepest aspirations, yearnings, and revelations to take subtle form within our consciousness to guide us to create new forms, new social structures, and organizations in the world. We become the future present, as they said about Jesus, claiming our inner potential as a reality, and allowing it to attract us forward to manifest in our lives.

Signs and Qualities of Youth

Following are some of the signs and qualities of our early Youth as I, and others, experience them presently. They can act as guideposts. Add your own signs as you experience yourself entering Youth.

We Are Achieving Continuity of Consciousness As Our Essential Selves

As we enter the phase of Youth, we can remember our identity most of the time. Just as early humans once stabilized self-consciousness in the midst of an animal world, so now young Universal Humans, at the very dawn of Universal Human history, are stabilizing Essential Self-awareness. Unitive consciousness is becoming a new norm. The illusion of separation rarely takes us over for long.

We find that the various gradients of self-awareness—body, mind, spirit—are flowing in a spectrum of consciousness so that we can operate fairly well at any level without separating from the other, ascending and descending at will.

We can meditate and lose all personal identity within the infinite, unconditional pure awareness; we can infuse the unique "pearl" of our personal essence with that divine intelligence, an aspect of the radiant bliss of the infinite self.

We can focus the Essential Self among the bevy of subpersonalities, egoic self-contractions, and addictive patterns that still remain from a lifetime of feeling separate, healing and making whole that which feels broken and in pain.

We can lift those weary selves up unto the peace of union with the Beloved until they forget themselves. Our local selves are our disciples. The are enjoying the pleasure of union and do not want to be separate any more.

We Are Coming into Form through Our Projects, Which Are Our Progeny, Our "Children"

In Youth, we begin to manifest our inner values in new projects, social innovations, books, works of art, organizations, political parties, enterprises, and institutions in every field that can actually assist in transforming our world. Instead of being limited by inappropriate structures, jobs, and relationships, we are actually creating aspects of the new social body. Our vocations bring forth elements of the new culture. Our genius codes are planted and flower as expressions of a new society realizing its own potential for conscious evolution.

In a sense, each of our genius codes is actually a vital element of the emerging social body, just as each cell is vital to the biological body. As we make our planetary transition, each person, each member of the social body, is awakened to new functions required for survival and growth now. We urgently need to develop better social processes to find the partners we long for who complement our own gifts. As we enter Youth, we need "vocationally oriented dating services" to help us discover our unique team. (One of the Foundation's projects is a Vocational-Dating Service for young Universal Humans!)

However, in the puberty of our Youth, even if we are manifesting our creativity in important projects, we are rarely, if ever, actually able to change the larger world en masse because most people are still unaware of the transition within themselves. Occasionally, an individual steps forward on the world scene as a great change agent.

Mikhail Gorbachev was such a person, but because he did not have a new culture to advocate, because he could only point to reformation of the failing communist system, or to the more attractive laissez-faire capitalism and individualistic democracy which was already showing its flaws and was not appropriate to the Russian culture, he could not complete his mission and was rejected. The former Soviet Union needed examples of cooperative, synergistic, win-win social models—models that have not yet been developed fully enough to serve the countries now in chaos and transition.

Nelson Mandela has perhaps done the best of any transitional Universal Human in the great work of overcoming apartheid in South Africa. Yet, like Gorbachev, the lingering problems that must be dealt with are so great that it is difficult for the new to emerge in the midst of life-threatening and egoic conflicts that remain unresolved.

New efforts are now forming, such as Ken Wilber's Integral Institute, which is bringing together leading theorists, activists, and creators in every major field, dedicated to "the integration of body, mind, soul, and spirit in self, culture, and nature."

The Buckminster Fuller Institute is developing a major website for "Humanity's Options for Success" (www.bfi.org).

The Institute of Noetic Sciences is linking up thousands in communities throughout the world (www.noetic.org).

Neale Donald Walsch's ReCreation Foundation teaches that the purpose of life is to "recreate ourselves anew in the next grandest version of the greatest vision we ever held about Who We Are." Its leading-edge program, Oneness Now (www.onenessnow.com), addresses a world-wide audience ready to seek ways to experience real unity, both with the Divine and with each other—which, says Walsch, "are one and the same thing."

In its Peace Room on the Internet and through the "Gateway to Our Conscious Evolution," the Foundation for Conscious Evolution is scanning for, mapping, connecting, and communicating with others whose work is transforming our world.

But these efforts, and many others of a similar kind, are, at this writing, still embryonic.

We Experience Vocational Arousal

In our biological phase of puberty our hormones turn on, our bodies change, we are moved passionately to find sexual partners and reproduce the species. So in our "second puberty" as Universal Humans, we are just as passionately aroused to find partners and join our genius to evolve ourselves. We move from self-reproduction to self-evolution.

The "essential hormones," as Suzanne Hubbard calls them in *The Life Book* (See page 183), awaken our passion to create. We shift from maximum, and often unchosen, procreation to co-creation. We may enter wild periods of "suprasexual promiscuity," where we want to fuse genius with anyone who is willing! We can't live up to our commitments. We suffer from "premature synergy" and can't remain in resonance long enough to actually create anything substantial together.

I can remember in the early days of my Youth going to conferences and meeting kindred souls. We would become vocationally aroused and stay up all night talking about how we were going to reform education, build a new political party, create a movie . . . and then, the next morning, we could hardly remember each others' names!

This sense of over-excitement and uncertainty can be frustrating and disorienting, especially if we are mature adults who have been successful in the existing culture. No matter how skilled we have been, when we enter the puberty phase of our Youth, our rational minds don't know what to do. We are reinventing our lives. This is good, for we are on the threshold of the unknown. As Dee Hock, founder of VISA International and author of *Birth of the Chaordic Age* (1999), told me the other day, "If we knew what to do, it wouldn't be it!"

Vocational arousal is the engine that fuels our natural evolution at this stage. In Youth, it becomes a dominant passion and an evolutionary driver for our own emergence. For as we attempt to come into form with our initiatives, we hit every possible obstacle within ourselves, as well as in the world. All our weak points show up.

If the desire to co-create is strong enough, we will persistently face every challenge as an opportunity to grow; we will continually transcend our self-imposed comfort limits and find that we are actualizing an immeasurable potential within ourselves. It is exhilarating and joyful. We are like great athletes working ourselves to the limit of our possibilities and then finding there is more to be revealed within ourselves.

A New Incentive to Free Ourselves
from Ego-Driven Behavior Arises

To actually join our genius, we must be relatively free of the illusion of separation. This illusion prevents the full fusion required for the next stage of liberation of untapped potentials. Co-creation requires that we complete the inner Emergence Process far enough to be aware when the ego enters in. For when it does, it destroys resonance and separates the two fusing geniuses. Then, the old power struggle of dominance and submission takes hold, and judgment and fear arise.

In Youth, we are freeing ourselves from the ego's usurpation of our creativity for its own insatiable needs. Let's be humble here. The ego does not immediately disappear. It is a lifelong process of self-education and the release of self-contractions.

As we mature, our creativity begins to flow more easily, less by competition and comparisons. Our acts are increasingly self-rewarding. They express us. They are self-rewarding. We feel rewarded in the doing and the being, therefore the impulse to feel driven and self-judgmental diminishes. We are transcending the dichotomy between selfish and selfless as we become self-evolving. Our greatest pleasure is our essential self-expression and the giving of our gifts to others in the world. Our most cherished reward is the freedom to be and do our best with others.

Our work is our life's expression unfolding in tangible form. Work is the process of creating, accessing our deeper genius, and joining with others in the dance of co-creation, an extension of the lover's dance of procreation. We are attracted and invigorated, energized and rejuvenated by our "work." In fact, our work is our cosmic connection with universal creativity.

At this stage of social life, we are rarely "hired" to perform our life purpose and must become co-creative entrepreneurs, often investing or paying our own money to do our work. We develop alternative economic innovations such as local currency, global barter, and many other such important ideas to support us in our emergence. We find this effort well worth it, because our life purpose expressed in chosen work is our passport to joy, companionship, fulfillment, and participation in the larger community of co-creative humans.

We Embark upon Co-creative Community

In Youth, we move beyond occasional meetings, at conferences, churches, and events, to the formation of extended chosen families and communities of shared purpose. We begin to participate in a continuous process of co-creation through specific projects and enterprises that provide opportunity for further unfoldment. Co-creative, sacred, human-scale communities begin to form. We need safe arenas to test out and experience the validity of our ideas and to stabilize our consciousness with others doing the same.

In biological evolution, mutations often occur among "isolates" that are separated from the mass of a given species. In social evolution, we need many "muddy pools," social laboratories that allow us to experiment and learn in a relatively harm-free and resonant field. Then as we mature, and as the social environment changes sufficiently to need new forms (as is happening right now due to the planetary crises), we can replicate what does work to enhance and evolve our lives.

This is already happening in obvious areas, such as in health and healing, where innovations that twenty years ago seemed impossible are commonplace, such as home births, midwives in hospitals, prayers in medical institutions, alternative and complementary therapies, and so forth.

We Experience Optimum Health and Regeneration

We begin to experience a sense of optimum well-being and increased energy that is a positive blessing. The combination of the alchemical process of inner union, combined with the stimulus of vocational arousal and co-creative work with others, activates the cells and infuses them with new life. Whatever age we are chronologically, as we enter Youth, we're flooded with energy that springs from the bliss of union and the passion to create. It is the sexual drive raised and extended into the suprasexual drive to move from maximum procreation to co-creation.

Sexuality itself is raised from its function of reproducing the species toward the new function of evolving ourselves through the union of the two as one.

There is a special function for post-menopausal women, I believe, perhaps since I am one! I remember so clearly when I was turning 50 and was going through menopause. One day, I was cleaning out my basement in Washington, D.C., when I heard a seductive inner voice whisper, "Would you like to die?" It was tempting and pleasant. I checked within and found, No, I've barely begun. "Would you like to get cancer, or would you like to rejuvenate?" the voice continued. I was shocked. "I had no idea that I had that choice," I responded internally. "Yes," the inner inspiration continued, "you do. Cancer is the body's panicked effort to grow without a plan. Rejuvenation occurs when you choose to activate the deeper design for your own evolution. The tendency toward cancer will be transformed into the regeneration of your cells as long as your willingness to fulfill your higher destiny continues. Death will become chosen when you are no longer willing to do so. You will live as long as you choose to create. Menopause leads to metamorphosis."

Now, at 70, twenty years later, I am amazed at the amount of energy that floods me every day. My strength is far greater than when I was 30, for at that time I was a seeker, I had not found my vocation or my community. My Essential Self was signaling discontent and frustration, but the guidance had not yet emerged. I was not "plugged in" to the larger design that now floods me with vitality moment by moment.

Now this creative energy heals me of most illnesses. I find I rarely get sick. I feel as though I am almost crossing over to a new life cycle.

I am not getting older, or younger, but rather newer every day. In fact, all of us over fifty are members of the newest generation on Earth. In the past we would have been dead! Now we are living from 50 to 60, 70, 80, as a new norm, feeling well, vigorous, and healthy. This is vital for the emergence of the Universal Human. It takes a long while to grow up.

We are not really new as teenagers or young people, because genuine newness requires that we find our vocations of destiny, make the shift from ego to essence, and gain our partners, resources, and venues in which to come into form. This is the meaning of longevity at this stage of our evolution. As elders from the future we are barely reaching the horizon far enough to cast our eyes forward into the unknown and come back with our reports to those climbing the mountain of conscious evolution.

We Surrender Our Separated Intentions

In our Youth, we cease seeking status or external rewards, even the achievement of specific goals. Yes, we have intentions, but these intentions seem to be part of a larger design of which we are intrinsic participants, rather than feeling that our own separate purposes must be achieved.

We find that as we surrender and let go of our egoic notion of the way things should be, we gain a far greater freedom, released from struggling and striving to win, enjoying the process and the product, just as the rest of nature does. Is a tree "achieving" something as it bursts into bloom in spring? Is a baby accomplishing a goal when it opens its eyes and smiles its first smile of recognition of its mother?

In fact, the ideas of achievement and success fade because we are self-rewarded. Abraham H. Maslow called this the "Eupsychian Society," the society of self-actualizing and self-transcending people, where the greatest reward is the freedom to do our work and where the highest pay is for those jobs that no one wants to do.

At this stage we are communing with other pioneering souls. We feel the union not only with those we know but with all those souls who are now drawn by their essence to emerge as Universal Humans, creating a vast planetary congregation from all faiths and cultures. We sense our common roots which go back to the beginning of time and then beneath time itself into the Void, Emptiness, the Source, the Ground of Being—God.

Once the taproot of our being permeates the infinite, the infinitesimal is radiant with eternity. We drink of the source that infuses our essence with itself, that source of which all of us are vital fountains, geysers of life expression.

That taproot sinks into the mind and heart of the cosmic creative wellspring of *that* out of which all existence rises and falls. The garden of our Youth, the Sunlit Garden of Co-Creation, is really the heart of God in the temporal world, the place where people "make love" manifest in form. Through procreative love we make babies. Through co-creative love we make worlds.

Part III.
Epilogue

We have come a long journey, yet this is just the beginning of our new lives and of our work in co-creating new worlds. We are a growing band of pioneering souls scattered in every culture, field, discipline, age, and background. We can have compassion upon all others and ourselves. We are very young and still fragile in our ability to stabilize our universal consciousness. What is new in us is so original and imperceptible that it is difficult to recognize what is emerging.

Our emergence as Universal Humans is a natural expression of the whole process of creation that brought existence from subatomic particles through matter, life, human life, and now us going around our turn of the spiral. What lies before us is unknown, magnificent beyond imaginings. But this much we can see. For fifteen billion years the universe has been rising in consciousness and freedom through greater complexity and synergy. Whatever is coming will be a further evolution in consciousness and freedom. This is the design of evolution. The only difference now is that we are conscious participants in it, of it, for it, as it.

It is my conviction that none of us can evolve fully into the stage of Adulthood until the collective culture is transformed. It is our work to help create the culture that can call forth Universal Humans in the future to be the kind of humans who can create this culture.

The challenge is huge and faces us on the social, planetary, and personal scale. It is vital for us to envision what it may be like when everything we know we can do *works* for the evolution of life. These kinds of visions become, as I have said, magnetic attractors to guide us in the use of our rapidly expanding capacities.

When and if we get through this very dangerous crisis of birth on the social scale, we can envision that we will have developed new kinds of social systems in every field—mind/body/spirit education, new approaches to health and healing, win-win forms of economics, self-organizing structures for our institutions, to name a few, which we can see emerging even now.

On the macrocosmic, planetary scale, we will have learned planetary ecological management and sustainable, regenerative economic development. In an Earth/Space expanded environment, we will have access to non-polluting, miniaturized technologies. These powers could transform the entire physical complex in which we live to one of sustainability, abundance, and unimaginable new powers, provided of course that we move beyond our egoic, collective misuse of these capacities.

On the individual or microcosmic scale, these new capacities will evolve the very life cycle of the Universal Human beyond the familiar mammalian sequence of conception, gestation, birth, puberty, reproduction, aging, and dying. We will undoubtedly reach a critical phase change in the animal life cycle when we creature humans will have learned to regenerate, to live in outer space, to transform our bodies to reflect our expanded consciousness and our new environments beyond our mother planet, to increase our intelligence to an exponential degree. At this next stage, we can imagine that the higher ranges of unitive consciousness, experienced even now by a growing number, will become a new norm. At this stage of consciousness, we experience the nature of reality as divine love/intelligence and will live out our identity as *that* in person, in touch with many dimensions of reality.

We can envision, based on the nature of the quantum transformations that preceded us, from pre-life to life, from animal life to human life, that the Adult Universal Human will emerge as something radically new yet inclusive of all that came before—an ever-evolving, co-creating, self-transforming cosmic human.

A profound question arises as to whether *Homo universalis* is the maturation of our own species, *Homo sapiens*, or the early stages of a new species. Here is my evolutionary intuition: We, *Homo sapiens*, are a cross-over generation out of which many "mutations" will come. We will self-evolve into a diversity of species. Some will continue to live on Earth and mature the lineage of *Homo sapiens*. Others will choose to live in space, change their bodies, and build many small worlds, travelling throughout the cosmos. Some of our new capacities, like nanotechnology, biotechnology, and supercomputing, may not be appropriate in a biosphere but may be vital for a universal species in outer space. Our metaphysical preferences will become evolutionary choices. As diversity decreases on Earth, we will gain diversity in the universe. The universe is the vast "wilderness," not the Earth. Mother Earth is giving birth to seeds of Earth life. When Father Sun expands and destroys all the planets in our solar system, as suns always do, billions of years hence, Earth's children will be galactic beings.

The third stage on our developmental path, Adulthood, leads not to old age and death, but rather to a transition to what might be called "universal life." This is an unknown. I envision that we will become cosmic beings, spanning the galaxies in cosmic consciousness, in touch with whatever other forms of life exist in the universe, as far beyond our current stage of *Homo sapiens sapiens* as we are from *Australopithecus africanus* millions of years ago. Project us forward even a few thousand years, let's say to the fourth millennium, a blink of the cosmic eye, and we can imagine the dim outlines of *Homo universalis*, a co-creator on a universal scale.

This is one person's vision. What is yours? As we are co-creators, it is very important what we envision, because, as I have said so often, our images of the future affect reality. As we see ourselves, so we act, and as we act so we tend to become. It is a participatory universe. There is freedom at the very core of reality. To be a conscious co-creator is not a metaphor; it is the power of metamorphosis. We are designed to know the design and to participate within it, as aspects of it, ourselves.

We are facing the unknown. Many great modern psychologists have prepared the way for our emergence as individual humans, but it hasn't been possible for anyone or any approach to fully chart this new path into the mature phases of Adulthood and beyond within a technologically enriched noosphere, because this expanded technological power of destruction and co-creation is radically new. The Universal Human we are becoming has not yet fully appeared, and so we can only point in the direction we are headed now.

To help us on our way, however, it is vital now that we develop self-images commensurate with the glorious possibilities of who we really are. The shining beauty of the young Universal Human potentiality is hardly ever seen in the arts, the films, the television, and the "news." Science fiction writers like Gene Roddenberry, Ray Bradbury, Arthur C. Clarke, and others have at least tried to give us some visions of ourselves in the future, but rarely are they attractive enough to motivate us to realize them. The media for the most part are portraying images of our failures, our weaknesses, our violent and tragic local selves. The daily "news" headlines are stories of our contending and anguished local selves. They are what Rev. Dr. Michael Beckwith calls "prayer requests."

We have not yet had our new portrait done. The Greek sculptors portrayed the beauty of young athletes and warriors, gods and goddesses, and a new image of humans was born. The medieval artists portrayed the Christ, the Virgin Mary, the Saints, giving us images of divinity, yet still seeing it as outside ourselves. Michelangelo sculpted the magnificent *David*, fully human and fully divine, yet he was unique, a hero beyond the so-called ordinary person. Modern art disintegrated this last great self-image that came forth in the Renaissance. We see ourselves broken up into points of light, new forms, streams of energy, the Void. The works of Monet, Manet, Pissarro, Picasso, Jackson Pollock, and the later great blank canvases of White-on-White revolutionized art in the modern period.

Now, our former self-images have all but disappeared. We are entering the *post* post modern period. Every past image has been deconstructed. I believe the most important artistic question now is, What are the new images of humans commensurate with our powers to shape the future? How can art, music, literature reveal us to ourselves, alive with the love and intelligence now radiantly conscious in ourselves, as a new norm, the next stage of human evolution? We call upon our artists to provide for us images, sounds, lights, words, poetry that evoke from us what we are becoming, that dramatize for us the Whole Story of Creation—so we can see ourselves being born as Universal Humans and a Universal Humanity. We need courage and encouragement to make the great transition.

All of us now attracted to the path of our own emergence should realize that we do not do this for ourselves alone, nor do we do it *as* ourselves alone. We are actually an expression of the Great Creating Process itself, finally expressing consciously through and as Universal Humans on planet Earth. The Essential Self is the personal expression of that Process incarnating in each of us, as us. Our maturation as Adult Universal Humans holds within it the fulfillment of the promise given to the human species through its great avatars, seers, and visionaries. We are to be the promise fulfilled, the end of a long struggle of life itself in the first chapter in the history of the world and the beginning of the second chapter which will tell the story of the appearance of new forms of life, co-creative with the process of evolution itself, never before seen on planet Earth.

Part IV.

Next Steps in the Emergence Process

Welcome to the community of universal sovereign persons now emerging everywhere. You are invited to enter a new arena of creativity and enjoyment that holds the promise of assisting in the transformation of ourselves and our world. In *Emergence* we have begun a lifelong process of shifting our identity from ego to essence and setting ourselves upon the developmental path of the Universal Human.

If you are practicing these ten steps, and if you have formed an Emergence Circle, you are already making a powerful contribution to self and social evolution. But obviously there is so much more. We are all at the beginning of our emergence. We are very young! The good news is that there are, throughout the world, teachings, trainings, organizations, institutes, books, and events that can assist us in our own evolution.

The Foundation for Conscious Evolution has designed a next step that connects the young Universal Human to the larger field of the emerging culture. It is called "The Entry Course: Gateway to Our Conscious Evolution." It is available on the Internet (www.peaceroom.org).

We invite you to enroll in the Gateway to Our Conscious Evolution. We also will be holding gatherings in Santa Barbara as well as other teachings and intensives to foster the formation of a world-wide community to support Universal Humans, wherever we may be. If you would like further information, you may visit our website at www.peaceroom.org or call (805) 884-9212.

The Entry Course: Gateway to Our Conscious Evolution

Step across the threshold, mighty pioneering souls of Earth! Here together we can fulfill the desire burning in our hearts for life ever-evolving, for love ever-expanding, for union with the divine within us, among us, and beyond us.

The Gateway is a living web leading you to ever-growing centers of creativity and love—people now transforming the world, offering a nexus of ideas, projects, and contacts to assist each of us in finding our heart's desire, our partners, and our greater life purpose, our vocations of destiny.

It is a doorway to the infinite, an opening into universal life on this Earth and far beyond.

The Gateway encompasses the range of experience we need as individuals and as communities in order to emerge as Universal Humans and join with others to co-create a world equal to our full potential. It consists of seven great themes. Each theme connects the learner with key practices, books, projects, teachers, social and spiritual innovators, and websites.

Seven Themes that Reveal our Potential for Conscious Evolution

The first theme offered is the *Whole Story of Creation*. We must know our new story, the miracle of our macrocosmic birth from the original act of creation to ourselves, the expression of fifteen billion years of success! We are the fruition of the great ordeal of existence and all forms of life. To them we bow down in humble awe and gratitude. We pledge that through us the sacrifice and genius of all that came before us will be fulfilled in the next step and that those who come after us will see us as a vital link in the chain of life that has led to life ever-evolving. As we learn the story, we realize we are the story come alive. We are actors in the play of creation. With what Brian Swimme (*Universe Story,* 1992) calls "comprehensive compassion" we extend our love to the whole community of life that has participated in its creation.

This subject covers the objective scientific story of our evolution from the void, through the origin of creation, the formation of matter, galaxies, planets, Earth, life, animal life, human life, and now ourselves going around the next turn of the evolutionary spiral. We study the latest views on the nature of reality and the universe coming forth from the new sciences.

We also discover the subjective aspect of the story, beginning with the new view of the universe as a living, interconnected, whole. We explore the evolutionary impulse, the "implicate order," as physicist David Bohm calls it. This tendency has been leading to higher consciousness and greater freedom through more complex order for billions of years. It has broken through in the consciousness of great beings of our species and is now, many of us believe, beginning to emerge as the motivation and love/intelligence of the Universal Human, that is, ourselves.

We understand that we are part of this great continuum of transformation now entering a phase change called *conscious* evolution. We are becoming conscious of the processes that are creating us—the atom, the gene, the brain. We are impacting our own evolution by everything we do. We must learn ethical evolution in time to save our world from our own misplaced egoic behavior. We humans are charged with bringing humaneness into evolution. Through our ability to love one another, we render the process of evolution loving. This is a transcendent task assigned to Universal Humanity for its own survival, for the well-being of Earth life, and for the glory of the whole process of creation, or God.

With our "evolutionary insight," we discover that we are entering the second chapter in the history of the world, awakening from the slumber of self-consciousness and preparing to take our natural roles as conscious participants with the process of creation. (See the Map of the First Two Chapters in the History of the World on page 178.)

Cosmogenesis, the story of cosmic evolution, provides us the momentum and majesty, the miracle and the mystery, of our own potential to evolve. Since we have, in fact, arisen from subatomic particles originated at the dawn of creation, who can even imagine what will be forthcoming from us at the dawn of co-creation, at the age of co-genesis, when we begin to co-generate new life forms and new worlds?

If this whole process is natural—and how could it be otherwise?—if it is natural for a big-brained intelligent species to understand the creative process and to identify with it as co-creators, then our future is vast, glorious, and indeed fulfills the profound longing in the human heart for greater meaning, purpose, and empowerment. If we are the only life in the vast universe of trillions of stars (which many scientists believe is unlikely), then we are indeed precious beyond imagining. If we are not alone, if there are innumerable other life forms emerging from their planetary wombs, then we are in for a tremendous quantum jump of learning at the point of contact. In either case, this is the most thrilling time to be born.

The Entry Course celebrates and humbly begins the task of learning how to co-evolve with nature and to co-create with the processes of creation.

From the fifteen-billion-year perspective, standing in the future, we can already foresee that our turn on the evolutionary spiral is leading toward higher consciousness and greater freedom through more complex order. We can see that the deepest aspirations of humanity for expanded life, for deeper union with Source, are at the very threshold of *coming true through evolving humans.*

The second theme in the Entry Course is the *Emergence of the Universal Human,* the subject of this book. We place the emerging human in the context of the larger story. We feel our own personal motivation as the evolutionary impulse urging us to evolve and express our creativity in the transformation of our culture. We sense that we are the universe in person, becoming self-aware and self-creating. In other words, we begin to flesh out within ourselves a new image of humans as co-creators. This is vital, for as we see ourselves, so we act, and as we act, so the world becomes. We commit to the practice of our own emergence as our primary purpose, realizing that from this all else follows. The participants find themselves connected to the Whole Story, as co-creators, in touch with others throughout the world.

The third theme is *Co-creative Relationships.* We draw upon the best teachers and practitioners of conscious relationship to learn to be with one another in love, essence with essence, beyond our personalities. We yearn to join not only our genes to have a child but our *genius* to give birth to one another and to the works that we can do together for the world. We explore the new relationship between women and men—the co-creative couple. As we shift from maximum procreation to co-creation and live longer lives, what is the purpose of our union? What are we meant to do and be as intimate, co-equal co-creators? What is the meaning of sexuality itself, when most love-making in the developed world is not to have a child? Is there greater meaning for our sexual union as we cross the threshold of *Homo sapiens* to *Homo universalis*? The Entry Course is an arena to explore these great questions.

We learn to move from dominance and submission to equality and co-creation. We cultivate resonance with one another so that we affirm and grow the Essential Self in each and support one another in educating the local selves. We learn to repattern our social lives—our intimate relationships, our families, our workplaces, and our communities—based on multiple "circles" of equals attuning to the heart of one another and leaving behind us the separating structures which no longer serve our evolution now.

Rich Ruster, co-founder of the Center of Co-Creation in Boulder describes co-creation: "To embody the co-creative activity consciously—from the inside out—is to live as the divine embodied and aware of itself at play" (*Voices of Conscious Evolution*, Vol. 1, Summer 2000).

The fourth component in the Entry Course is *Co-creative Vocation*. As we gain deeper resonance with one another, our unique creativity is stimulated. Just as each of us has a genetic code guiding the formation of our physical bodies, so each has a genius code, the blueprint of our potential talents and gifts that yearn now to be expressed. Everyone wants, above all, to be free to give their gift, to make their contribution. As it is stated in the Gospel of Thomas: *"If you bring forth what is within you, what you bring forth will save you. If you do not bring forth what is within you, what you do not bring forth will destroy you."*

The genius code is the "entelechy," from the Greek, meaning "the condition of a thing whose essence is fully realized; actuality as distinguished from potentiality; a vital force urging an organism toward self-fulfillment" (The American Dictionary, 2ⁿᵈ Edition). Our entelechy is the oak pressing within the acorn to become a mighty tree. It is the power of the delicate green shoot breaking through the frozen ground in Spring. It is the butterfly silently self-organizing while hidden in the disintegrating caterpillar.

By accessing and expressing these genius codes through our calling—our soul's code, as James Hillman has described it—while releasing ourselves from bondage to our egoic personalities, we become co-creative humans in the world. Vocational arousal, the desire to self-actualize through chosen self-expression, is the fuel that drives us to undergo the arduous process of Essential Self-education. In my experience, the passion to give our gift, rather than idealism, ambition, or guilt, is the personal evolutionary driver that has the energy to break the bonds of limited self-centered consciousness. Sexual passion empowered us to overcome great challenges to join with each other to reproduce the species—a heroic task when you consider the difficulty of raising children in the early human world. So now, I believe, the *suprasexual* drive to express our creativity will give us the energy to overcome our own limitations, to join with one another to co-create beyond our egos, to self-evolve rather than to self-reproduce.

In the Entry Course, and through other teachings and gatherings, we gain access to our "vocations of destiny" and connect with guides, mentors, and leaders at the growing edge of change. We grow and enlarge ourselves, joining in greater synergy with many others. We transcend our separated individualism and become even more individuated by becoming an integral part of a larger whole. Union differentiates. Synergy creates newness. Here we draw upon *The Co-creator's Handbook* as a prime tool for this theme.

Co-creative Community is the fifth theme, focusing on the formation of human-scaled, sacred community. How do we come together as young Universal Humans to co-create a new culture based on our own values and desires? We are learning here the next stage of human self-organization and participating in the evolution of democracy itself. All throughout the world there are now social experiments in living together as co-creative humans. Networks of communities are being formed.

I am a co-founder of such a community in Santa Barbara. All that was necessary was to publicly ask the question, *What would happen if this community experienced its own potential for conscious evolution?* to draw together those in whom this question is already alive and begin an experiment as a community dedicated to self and social evolution.

We believe that in every community individuals like ourselves can put out the call and gather together and support one another in creating in microcosm the world we choose. Through community-building endeavors, we seed the larger world with social well-being and new models of co-creative life styles. We reconnect with our indigenous roots, which have almost been lost in the modern world, as well as using the most advanced modern technologies. It is in the context of co-creative relationships and community that the Universal Human can be nurtured and matured.

The Santa Barbara Conscious Evolution Community stands ready to be of assistance to others in this great endeavor as we learn and teach ourselves. We are calling on social transformational leaders like Dee Hock, founder of VISA International, with his Chaordic Design Process, which we are applying in the formation of our own community. In his book, *Birth of the Chaordic Age* (1999), he defines "chaordic" as: "*1. The behavior of any self-governing organism or system which harmoniously blends characteristics of order and chaos. 2. Patterned in a way dominated by neither chaos nor order. 3. Characteristic of the fundamental organizing principles of evolution and nature.*" His organization, the Chaordic

Alliance, is serving organizations of all kinds throughout the world to repattern to a higher level of synergistic order.

Dee says about community: "Our current forms of organization are almost universally based on compelled behavior—on tyranny—for that is what compelled behavior is, no matter how benign it may appear or how carefully disguised and exercised. The organization of the future will be the embodiment of community based on shared purpose calling to the higher aspirations of people."

We are also learning from Don Beck, author with Christopher C. Cowan of *Spiral Dynamics: Mastering Values, Leadership, and Change* (1996). He writes:

> When a new human form occurs, whether a new pattern of behavior or a new vMEME [self-replicating value system] certain mutant forms usually appear before the new "habit" sticks. These may arise over a period of years or centuries. Eventually, a new critical mass must gather to ensure that almost everyone is doing it, or being it. Then the novel becomes the norm.
> . . . At our present stage in human development the Turquoise vMEME [What Don calls the eighth stage of social evolution, such as is arising in Santa Barbara] is at an embryonic stage. While a few of our ancestors may have meditated over it for five thousand years, a clear and concise picture has still not emerged from the developing fluids of time. However, certain important "holons" have become evident as this eighth vMEME metabolizes in the mist and becomes a force to be reckoned with.

We are discovering that by being together we establish a "resonant field" which *feels* as though we are being connected at a deeper level with a cosmic pattern. It is a field of *agape*, or love. We stop having to figure things out, sometimes becoming quiet, noticing that what we have been striving for is what we already are. A peace descends among us. It is impossible to explain this by intellectual means, but it is palpable. I believe it is the social aspect of the inner experience that occurs when the local selves join the Beloved in the heart. We are co-creating a social Rose Chamber of Union, spontaneously, without fully knowing what we are doing. It is a morphogenetic field, an invisible, non-physical field that is composed of the behavior of all the entities involved, as described by Rupert Sheldrake. The people involved are not spiritual adepts, but rather teachers, artists, business executives, coaches, musicians, parents, scientists. No one is the leader, although I was initially a catalyst for its formation. It is becoming self-organizing.

We are seeking to create conditions for social synergy, so that each of us can express our creativity through joining with others for the good of the self and the community as a whole. We aim at a triple-win: win for the person, win for others, and win for the larger design of creation of which we are all manifestations.

As we once learned Robert's Rules of Order for parliamentary procedure, now we learn synergistic rules of order. These are win-win-win rules where each person is valued, precious, and responsible to give his or her gifts within the whole. We expand upon Thomas Jefferson's Declaration of Independence to create the new Declaration of Co-Creation, which opens as follows:

> We hold these truths to be self-evident,
> that all people are born creative,
> endowed by our Creator
> with the inalienable opportunity and responsibility
> to express our creativity
> for the good of ourselves, our families, our communities, and our society as a whole.

This brings us to the sixth theme of the Entry Course, *Co-creative Society.* This new society is being formed even now by social, spiritual and technological innovations, networks, organizations, and activities emerging in every field and function. (See diagram of the Wheel of Co-Creation, page 177.) But due to the scattered nature of the innovations, and the fact that our mass media, political system, and popular culture hardly recognize these innovations, we often do not even know they exist. Although the subculture of "Cultural Creatives" is large and growing in the United States and throughout the world, wherever people have freedom, opportunity, education, and economic development, most of us still think we are alone. We have not yet had a mirror to see ourselves as the emerging species that we are, nor to connect and to co-create.

For this great theme we draw from the model of the global Peace Room on the Internet as developed by The Foundation for Conscious Evolution. The Peace Room is to become as sophisticated as our world governments' war rooms, where we track enemies and strategize how to defeat them. In our Peace Rooms on the Internet and in local communities person to person, we learn how to map our innovations in every field and function and work together to realize the full potential of the whole system. (See *Conscious Evolution: Awakening the Power of Our Social Potential.*)

In the Entry Course, and through the larger work of the Foundation for Conscious Evolution, we co-create this Peace Room process, so that each of us will be assisted in finding where our unique genius fits and where our gifts are most needed. Here we learn from "quantum innovations," key projects now transforming our system, leading us toward the next stage of evolution. We study what is working. From this new pragmatic base, we discover the design of social evolution. Out of this design there emerges an Evolutionary Agenda—those acts that we can now do, and are in fact doing—which together can carry us through this crises toward the next stage of our evolution.

The seventh and final theme in the Entry Course is called *Visions of a Universal Humanity*. Here we envision the next stage of our collective as well as our personal evolution. We see this next stage as a great magnet in which to place our visions, intuitions, choices, and commitments for our full emergence as a Universal Humanity. These visions are inherent in the human psyche. They have arisen throughout all of history as mystical revelation, artistic intuition, as well as scientific imagination. Now these visions can be seen as the next set of real possibilities of our actual evolution based on the harmonious use of our spiritual, social, and scientific/technological capacities—a quantum jump as great as from pre-life to life, or animal life to human life. If we connect the peaks of human performance and imagine them as the basis for the new norm, we can catch a glimpse of ourselves evolved. Such positive images of our future once held in common will attract us to fulfill them. Whatever image we hold of our own future becomes a self-fulfilling prophecy.

Now that you have been given a brief overview of the Entry Course, imagine yourself as an individual student journeying through this course of study in your life. You are drawn in by a passionate evolutionary impulse in the heart to be more fully expressed in the world. As you learn the magnificent story of our creation, you discover that, lo and behold, you are a vital participant in the drama, you are needed, and you are connected to others you need.

Then imagine yourself deepening your relationships, joining essence with essence, first within yourself, so that the Essential Self is at home in the household of selves, then with others doing the same. There is a joy and even ecstasy in this experience which floods you with the vitality and light needed to continue on your evolutionary journey.

Then you awaken to your true life purpose, your vocation of destiny which can only be discovered in the "field" of others whose life purposes fit your own. You cannot give your best in a world that does not want it. Feel the joy of co-creating, of uniting in spiritual intimacy with others, fusing genius, exploding with dormant creativity. See yourself connecting with emerging leaders and serving those who are paving the way, thereby bringing forth your vocation into the world effectively.

Now you are a co-creator. Place your vision of Universal Humanity in the next turn of the spiral. Reach out, and up and onward, until you feel your hands touching the stars, while your mind is penetrating the veil of matter to fuse with the universal source of creation, and the bud of your desire is unfurling in form, flowering and fulfilling your heart's desire.

Is this idealistic? Well, no more so than that a single cell uniting with others to become a fish, a reptile, a bird. No more incredible than *Australopithecus africanus* becoming *Homo habilis*, *Homo erectus*, *Homo Neanderthalensis*, and finally *Homo sapiens*. No more unrealistic than you emerging out of your humanness to become a Universal Human. It's all a mystery, all awesome beyond words. Yet it all happened, improbable as it may seem. Why would we suppose that the process would stop here, with us, a furry biped with an eternally questing spirit and a love too great to be contained by the self-centered mind?

The Entry Course will be an evolving, open-ended journey into the growing edge of people now creating a new world.

Part V.
Resource Section

If Emergence *has resonated with the truth in your own heart, I suggest you go back to the beginning of the Guide and begin the process in depth. Then join with a global community in the Entry Course: Gateway to Our Conscious Evolution by enrolling now.*

Glossary

Co-creator:

A synonym for Universal Human. In a co-creator, individual creativity is aligned with, inspired by, and guided by the deeper patterns of creation, the implicate order, the tendency in evolution for higher consciousness and greater freedom through more complex order. In traditional religious terms, the co-creator freely surrenders the separated will to the will of God, becoming god-in-action in the world.

Essential Self:

The Essential Self resides at the core of our being, manifesting the qualities of wholeness, freedom, love, autonomy that the local self seeks through manipulating the external world. It is our higher self, or God-self. The Essential Self is the unique expression of the larger design of creation, non-dual Reality, the mind of God. It is the unique expression of the divine that holds the "entelechy," or fulfillment of the Universal Human that each of us is. When the local self is lifted up into the vibratory field of the Essential Self, it releases its patterns, disappears, and reappears as the active elements of the integrated human, the whole being, the Universal Human. The Essential Self is realized as the source of the unique guidance and inspiration each of us receives. As we incarnate as the Essential Self we are able to say, "I am the voice I hear. I am the guide who guides me. I am the Beloved I seek." Our goal is the full incarnation of essence as ourselves in resonance with the larger reality of the whole (God, Source, Spirit), other essential selves, and nature itself. There are many words used for the Essential Self, such as higher self, deep self, God-self, Christ-self.

The work and teachings of A. H. Almaas, especially in his book *Essence* (1986), have inspired the choice of the word "essence":

> The central aspect of essence is what we call the personal essence. The personal aspect of essence is actually the true essential personality. It is the person. It is experienced as oneself. The sense is of oneself as a precious being. There is then fullness, completeness, and contentment. It is as if the individual feels full and complete, realized. Nothing is lacking. No more search, any desire of wanting anything else. The person feels "now I have myself. I am a complete individual. I am fullness."

Genius Code:

As each of us has a genetic code, so we also have a genius code. This code is the seed of our unique creativity, talent, and personal expression that yearns to come into form in the world. When we become "vocationally aroused," the genius code awakens and passionately desires to express itself in the world. It expresses our personal essence coming into form, not as a driven local self seeking success but a unified whole self naturally expressing itself. (The work of the aroused genius is self-rewarding and fulfilling in itself.) The genius code is a source of motivation as great as the sexual drive to reproduce and procreate. It manifests a "suprasexual" drive to self-evolve and to co-create, to give its gift into the world, through joining genius with others. It is the great motivator of each of us to take the steps required to become a Universal Human, from Infancy through Childhood, Youth, Adulthood, and beyond. When the genius code is freed from ego and attachment, it flows with spontaneous creativity that transforms our world. The ego then becomes the servant of the personal essence and genius code, fulfilling its heart's desire through union with the inner divine. Our faith is that each person's genius code is actually needed in the evolution of the world and holds a vital code in the emerging social body.

God:

As we gain the powers we used to attribute to our gods through the noosphere, we shift our relationship to God from being children to being heirs and partners—very young, newly born co-creators, designed to participate consciously in the process of creation, first on this Earth, then in the universe beyond. The word God evolves in the first age of conscious evolution from external deity, patriarch, Father, to the Great Creating Process Itself now breaking through into human consciousness as our motivation to co-create and self-evolve. It is the "mother universe," the ground of being, the non-dual Reality, and the "prime directive" of evolution that animates every particle with intelligence and the desire to prevail, survive, and transcend every limit to life ever-evolving. It is the source of the continuous creation of the universe and the very quintessence of our personal essence. Through our shift of identify from ego to essence, we overcome the illusion of separation of the human from the divine, for we are incarnating the presence of the divine as ourselves. Synonyms: Source, Spirit, Creative Intelligence, Cosmic Design.

Local Self:

The personality, egoic self that may seek higher guidance, may receive signals from inner voices and spiritual masters, and have unitive flashes of deeper contact with source, yet feels separate from that guidance, driven, desirous of satisfaction, but unable to achieve inner peace or true rest. There are many sub-personalities within the local self encompassing a range of experiences, such as anxiety, lack of self worth, fear, jealousy, possessiveness. From the point of view of *Emergence*, the root cause of all these experiences is the illusion of separation from the source of our being, or from the divine essence that each of us is. The ego is not "bad," nor is it an entity, but rather patterns of reactivity and self-contraction that become ingrained because of the illusion of separation from source. Ego actually longs for union with essence. This union is its only true heart's desire and only refuge and fulfillment. Given the new powers of humanity, especially in the military/technological/industrial complex, it is no longer feasible to have the control of these capacities in our collective egoic personalities who tend to use these powers for self-centered purposes leading to global breakdown, and even the extinction of human civilization.

Noosphere:

The thinking layer of Earth composed of our planetary consciousness, formed from our language, our religions, our arts, culture, our laws, constitutions, institutions, and more recently our vast technological powers. These capacities collectively give humans the power of gods. In it lies the powers of co-destruction or co-creation. It must be guided by Universal Humans in attunement with the deeper patterns of nature, or the noosphere could be the vehicle of our self-destruction and extinction.

Universal Human:

The Universal Human is the integrated whole being whose Essential Self is in dominion within the household of local selves. In the Universal Human, the genius code is awakened and the person is beginning to express in the world as a conscious co-creator of the world. The Universal Human lives in an expanded cosmic consciousness, feels connected to the whole (God, Source, Spirit, Life) as well as to the individual part that each one is. This kind of human is motivated by spirit to express life purpose and is filled with love, enthusiasm, and the vibrant expression of the divine. The Universal Human is a forebear of *Homo universalis* who will carry the seed of Earth life far into the unknown realms of the universe of both inner space and outer space. The Universal Human is emerging en masse during the time of the planetary crisis when *Homo sapiens* gains the power of co-destruction and co-creation. This emerging type holds within its nature the survival and transformation of the world at this stage of evolution.

Universal Humanity:

Universal Humanity is the collective culture formed by Universal Humans who live in an enriched noosphere which holds the capacity for radical transformation of the material world, including the physical body. A Universal Humanity would be guided by Universal Humans to apply new social/technological capacities or possibilities such as nanotechnology, biotechnology, quantum computing, zero-point energy, appropriately for the enhancement of Earth life, the restoration of Earth, and the exploration of the solar system and beyond. Universal Humanity is the culture that will carry the seed of Earth life into an immeasurable future far beyond the confines of this cross-over generation.

Conscious Evolution Library

Adi Da, *The Dawn Horse Testament of Heart*. The Adidam Emporium, Lake County, CA 95461. To order online: www.adidam.com.

Almaas, A. H. 1986. *Essence: The Diamond Approach to Inner Realization*. York Beach, ME: Samuel Weiser, Inc.

Anderson, Carolyn, and Katharine Roske. *The Co-creator's Handbook: An Experiential Guide to Discovering and Fulfilling Your Soul's Purpose*. Website: www.global family.net

Aurobindo, Sri. 1998. *The Human Cycle: The Psychology of Social Development*. Twin Lakes, WI: Lotus Light Pub.

Beck, Don Edward, and Christopher C. Cowan. 1996. *Spiral Dynamics: Mastering Values, Leadership and Change*. Cambridge, MA: Blackwell Business.

Bolen, Jean Shinoda, M.D. 1999. *The Millionth Circle: How to Change Ourselves and the World. The Essential Guide to Women's Circles*. Berkeley, CA: Conari Press.

Bruteau, Beatrice. 1997. *God's Ecstasy: The Creation of a Self-Creating World*. New York: The Crossroad Publishing Co.

Chaisson, Eric. 1987. *The Life Era: Cosmic Selection and Conscious Evolution*. New York: Atlantic Monthly Press.

Elgin, Duane. 1993. *Awakening Earth: Exploring the Human Dimensions of Evolution*. New York: Morrow.

————. 2000. *The Promise Ahead: Humanity's Journey from Adolescence to Adulthood*. New York: Morrow.

Henderson, Hazel. 1996. *Building a Win-Win World: Life Beyond Global Economic Warfare*. San Francisco: Berrett-Koehler Publishers, Inc.

Hock, Dee. 1999. *Birth of the Chaordic Age*. San Francisco: Berrett-Koehler Publishers, Inc.

Houston, Jean. 2000. *Jump Time: Shaping Your Future in a World of Radical Change*. New York: J. P. Tarcher/Putnam.

Jung, Carl. 1969. *Synchronicity: An Acausal Connecting Principle*. Princeton, NJ: Princeton University Press.

Kurzweil, Ray. 1999. *The Age of Spiritual Machines: When Computers Exceed Human Intelligence*. New York: Viking.

Morrissey, Mary Manin. 1996. *Building Your Field of Dreams*. New York: Bantam Books.

———. 2001. *No Less than Greatness*. New York: Bantam Books.

Pert, Candace B. 1997. *Molecules of Emotion: The Science Behind Mind Body Medicine*. New York: Simon & Schuster.

Ray, Paul H., Ph.D., and Sherry Ruth Anderson, Ph.D. 2000. *The Cultural Creatives: How 50 Million People Are Changing the World*. New York: Harmony Books.

Redfield, James. 1995. *The Celestine Prophecy: An Adventure*. New York: Warner Books.

———. 1997. *The Celestine Vision: Living the New Spiritual Awareness*. New York: Warner Books.

———. 1996. *The Tenth Insight: Holding the Vision*. New York: Warner Books.

Russell, Peter. 1995. *The Global Brain Awakens: Our Next Evolutionary Leap*. Palo Alto, CA: Global Brain, Inc.

———. 1999. *From Science to God: The Mystery of Consciousness and the Meaning of Light*. Sausalito, CA: Peter Russell.

Swimme, Brian, and Thomas Berry. 1992. *The Universe Story: From the Primordial Flaring Forth to the Ecozoic Era*. New York: HarperCollins.

Wade, Jenny. 1996. *Changes of Mind: A Holonomic Theory*

of the Evolution of Consciousness. New York: State University of New York Press.

Walsch, Neale Donald. 1995. *Conversations with God: An Uncommon Dialogue, Book 1.* New York: G. P. Putnam's Sons.

———. 1997. *Conversations with God: An Uncommon Dialogue, Book 2.* Charlottesville, VA: Hampton Roads Publishing Co., Inc.

———. 1998. *Conversations with God: An Uncommon Dialogue, Book 3.* Charlottesville, VA: Hampton Roads Publishing Co., Inc.

———. 1999. *Friendship with God: An Uncommon Dialogue.* New York: Random House.

———. 2000. *Communion with God.* New York: Putnam's Sons.

Wilber, Ken. 1996. *A Brief History of Everything.* Boston: Shambhala.

———. 1996. *One Taste: The Journals of Ken Wilber.* Boston: Shambhala.

Zukav, Gary. 1990. *The Seat of the Soul.* New York: Simon & Schuster.

Books by Barbara Marx Hubbard:

Conscious Evolution: Awakening the Power of Our Social Potential. 1998. Novato, CA: New World Library.

The Revelation: A Message of Hope for the New Millennium. 1995. Novato, CA: Nataraj Pub.

The Hunger of Eve: One Woman's Odyssey Toward the Future. 1989. Eastsound, WA: Island Pacific Northwest. (To be ordered from The Foundation for Conscious Evolution.)

The Evolutionary Journey. 1982. (To be ordered from The Foundation for Conscious Evolution.)

REFERENCES

p. 68: Jacotte Chollet, Multidimensional Music. MMD Productions, BP 56, Lamorlaye 60260. France. Website: www.multidimensionalmusic.com.

p. 136: Ken Wilber's Integral Institute. Contact Leonard Jacobs, Shambhala Publications, 300 Massachusetts Avenue, Boston, MA 02115

p. 136: Buckminster Fuller Institute. "Advancing Humanity's Option for Success." Website: www.bfi.org.

p. 137: Institute of Noetic Sciences, 101 San Antonio Road, Petaluma, CA 94952. Tel. 707-775-3500.

p. 137: ReCreation Foundation. Its leading-edge program, Oneness Now, is at www.onenessnow.com.

p. 138, 160: Dee Hock's website: www.chaordic.org.

The Wheel of Co-Creation

177

The Story of the Birth of Universal Humanity

Map of the First Two Chapters in the History of the World

The Field out of which everything is co-arising:
The Void. The Great Mystery. The mind of God.
Source. Spirit. Ground of Being. Mother Universe. Light.
The Prime Directive toward which everything is arising:
Higher consciousness and greater freedom
through more complex cooperative order.

Chapter One

15 billion years ago: Our Universe flares forth
           QUANTUM JUMP

4.5 billion years ago: Our Earth forms
           QUANTUM JUMP

3.5 billion years ago: Life appears
           QUANTUM JUMP
2-3 million years ago: *Australopithecus africanus,*

Homo habilis,
Homo erectus,
Neanderthalensis

QUANTUM JUMP

Dawn of Human History

200,000-50,000 years ago . . . .*Homo sapiens* emerges older cultures—tribal, egalitarian

35,000 years ago . . . . .Self reflective, self consciousness arises

10,000 years ago . . . . .Agriculture, village, farming

5,000 years ago . . . . .City state, civilization

2,500 years ago . . . . .Buddha - Enlightenment

2,000 years ago . . . . .Jesus - Incarnation

"You shall do the works that I do and even greater works than these shall you do."

"Behold I show you a mystery: We shall not all sleep but we shall all be changed . . . "

300 years ago to present . . . . .The evolution of science and democracy: tools of transformation.

The evolution of religion: Shift in our relationship to God leading towards incarnation as co-creators— Emerson, Aurobindo and the Mother, Teilhard de Chardin, Ernest Holmes, Charles and Myrtle Filmore, and others.

Period of Transition to the Second Chapter in the History of the World

1945
- Based on Einstein's discovery that $E = MC^2$, we penetrate nature's invisible technologies of creation. The United States builds the first atomic bombs and drops them on Japan. The signal that self-conscious humanity with this much power could destroy the world.
- Global Ethic towards peace emerges

1950s
- Discovery of the language of the genetic code
- Development of computers
- Development of contraceptives

1960s
- Apollo lunar landing: Humans step upon a new world. We become physically universal. Picture of Earth from space
- Environmental awareness awakens
- Global ethics toward sustainability and interconnectivity
- Women seek identity, equality—shift from maximum procreation to cocreation
- Human and spiritual potential movements
- Mind expanding substances and experiences
- Social movements for peace, human rights, civil rights, social justice, etc.

1970s
2000
&
beyond
- No vision of our future equal to our new powers
- Few social forms for the expanded consciousness
- Reactivity, confusion, awareness of possible environmental collapse
- Ultimate evolutionary driver fear of extinction caused by our self-centered behavior
- Ultimate evolutionary attractor - possibility of our own transformation

Chapter Two—Dawn of Universal Human History
Timeframe: 2000-2050

MACROCOSMIC	MESOCOSMIC	MICROCOSMIC

QUANTUM BREAKDOWNS

Planetary shift	Social Shift	Personal Shift
Pollution, over population, resource depletion, nuclear proliferation, threat of environmental collapse within 30-50 years	Widening gap between rich and poor, economic instability, failure of institutions to meet new challenges; commercialization, loss of family, community, identity, etc.	Alienation, violence, sense of meaninglessness, depression, etc.

NOT SUSTAINABLE / TIME CRITICAL
Problems cannot be resolved in the same state of consciousness in which they are created nor by linear steps alone.

QUANTUM BREAKTHROUGHS
Quantum Transformation-capacities that lead to radical newness

Conscious ethical evolution begins • The evolution of evolution from unconscious to conscious participation • Learning planetary ecological management *Evolutionary Technologies* • Zero point energy • Supercomputers • Nanotechnology • Space Development • Life Extension • Bio-energetic, sound and light healing Moving beyond the Newtonian mechanistic universe towards the "Living Universe" interconnectivness, continuous creation, participatory, growing beyond scarcity and the creature human life cycle, etc.	*Synergy among social innovations* emerging in every field. (The Peace Room) *Synergistic Self-Organization* as in Chaordic Design and Synergistic Convergence *Evolutionary Agenda* emerges based on real options for humanity's long term success in alignment with natural systems *New News* the media begins to carry the stories of humanity's effort to survive and evolve, etc.	*The crossover generation* • The Universal Human emerges en masse • Mystical and secular consciousness merge in the cocreator **The New Developmental Path** *Gestation and Birth* • First awakenings • Vocational arousal • Choice to move beyond egoic personality *Infancy* • Essential self takes dominion • The bliss of union *Childhood* • Shift from ego to essence • Transferring authority • Educating local selves • Repatterning our life *Youth* • Continuity of essential self-consciousness • Coming into form through projects • Formation of cocreative organizations • Reformation of society

Quantum Transformation Achieved
We are born as a Universal Humanity
Timeframe: 2050-4000?

Our crisis is a birth, Mother Earth is giving birth to a species
capable of metamorphosis. We are the cross-over generation
between *Homo sapiens* and *Homo universalis*.

MACROCOSMIC	MESOCOSMIC	MICROCOSMIC
Quantum technologies operative	Memetic code shifts to the new paradigm— holistic, global/universal, spiritually attuned to a unified force and guiding principles that set the course of the universe with which we align. Win-win-win social systems create synergy on Earth leading to a jump in consciousness and freedom.	Adult Universal Human emerges, capable of attuning to the deeper patterns of creation and guiding the powers of the noosphere towards universal life on Earth and beyond
Shared contact with other life?		
Intergalactic Travel		
Transhuman life forms through extended capacities.		Cosmic Consciousness

Universal Humanity Emerges

When the Sun expands and destroys all the
planets in our solar system, we will be galactic
beings, co-creative on a universal scale.

The Life Book:
The Blueprint

Suzanne Hubbard

Suzanne identifies the conception, gestation, and birth of the Universal Human in *The Life Book* (what I have called the first stage). As you can see, we are in the early phases of mapping our developmental path. There will be many such efforts until the generic outlines are clear, as they are now with the developmental process of biological organisms.

We reprint here an excerpt titled "The Blueprint" containing key concepts both to support the reader's emergence and to prepare the way for *The Life Book* when it is ready. (For further information write to Suzanne Hubbard, 60 Walnut Ave., Takoma Park, MD 20912.)

THE BLUEPRINT

Stage One: Local Self, Essential Self

When we are born . . . as a physical child we are . . . endowed with two qualities of being. . . . We are the local self who is the biological, ego, personality self, and we are also the Essential Self, the nonlocal self which is resonant with the larger reality, the mind of God.

The local self represents the part of our being which is referred to as our human nature. It is the part of us that feels threatened and vulnerable. Local attitudes associated with human nature become triggered when our personal self feels threatened in any way. It is human nature to align with a physical reality based on survival of the fittest. If we continue reinforcing a hostile reality based on survival of the fittest, our hostility will ultimately become the biggest threat to our physical survival. The emergence of Universal Humans signifies that a maturation process is ready to take place. We are reprogramming our instincts and realigning our attitudes with a new framework of understanding, based on expanded awareness of our Essential Self. As a Universal Human, the local self becomes the emissary and implementer of essential levels of awareness evoked from the Essential Self. The evolutionary process transubstantiates an existence based on survival of the fittest to an existence that recognizes that we are all one at the essential level.

Encoded within the Essential Self is an inner potential, or *genius code*. Both the Essential Self and the genius code are receptive to nonlocal, resonant forms, or fields of consciousness. The Essential Self is the substance through which we access the unlimited domain of the Larger Whole.

Our genius code accesses fields of consciousness associated with archetypal ancestors. Experienced as nonlocal memory, the genius code evokes "knowings"—understandings and perspectives originally brought into consciousness by our ancestors.

In general, we are unconscious of the Essential Self. The evolutionary journey of a Universal Human begins the process of unfolding that awakens us to our inner being.

Stage Two: Unitive Experiences

A unitive experience signifies the initial sense of interconnectedness with what feels like an intentional universe. Suddenly our deeper and even hidden desire for greater awareness and more life resonates with the pattern of universal evolution. We are infused with a unique sense of vitality. An unconscious feeling of interconnection with the larger whole, with transcendent reality occurs, evoking a sense of joy, harmony, energy, and light, an awareness of immortality, a sense of expectancy, as well as a feeling of oneness filled with divine grace.

Unitive experiences are annunciations of one's "genius code," or inner potential. The annunciation cultivates the local self in preparation for a consciousness awakening further down the evolutionary path. The local self becomes imprinted with these peak experiences. Once imprinted, the local self "remembers" its own higher self and desires to recapture the experience, unless it is rendered fearful by external authorities that deny the reality of these experiences.

Stage Three: Landmarks, Signposts, and Pivotal Moments

The evolutionary journey and the physical journey of the local self run parallel to each other. Once imprinted with unitive experiences, we unconsciously seek to recapture the experience of union and interconnectedness.

There is a discordant relationship between the two paths that often unbalances the local self. The local self gets thrown off balance and leaves the external or normal life path, falling into unknown territory . . . a threshold of discovery. We become aware of an inner path. Life's upheavals are conduits to deeper levels of awareness. Emotional upheavals, disappointments, and life-challenging situations become evolutionary events that provide the conditions that open our awareness to an inner path. We may attune to the Essential Self for the first time.

The vulnerability that occurs during emotional situations opens up new levels of awareness, revealing an inner path. Once revealed, this path evokes a sense of higher destiny. . . . The local self recognizes a new direction and may become aware of deeper patterns, an "implicate order," the "prime directive" of evolution toward higher consciousness and greater freedom. We begin to feel a source of guidance.

Stage Four: The Point Where Conscious Evolution Begins

Once we become aware of an inner path, our external and inner paths intersect. A crossroad is reached in the evolutionary process. This is a place of choice. One can use expanded levels of awareness only as a therapeutic way of coping with life's ups and downs, or apply the expanded awareness to manifest an expansive life. The choice is to adapt to our own limits, or to consciously choose to self-evolve. The inner path becomes a generic evolutionary highway, guiding those who seek to participate in their developmental process. The new path opening up is not a private path but a transitional bridge open to anyone who wishes to evolve. As we cross over, we enter the pre-dawn of Universal Human history. The opening lines of a new story are inscribed within our hearts. We write the first lines as we embark consciously on the evolutionary journey.

Identification with the physical nature of the local self begins to erode. The substance of the Essential Self feels more substantial, and the patterns of the larger whole feel more real. Essential self-guidance is felt more frequently. We desire the opportunity to experience "deep witnessing" of our essential qualities. We wish to self-recognize as well as be recognized by others for our inner qualities.

This is the threshold that marks a departure from an existence aligned with the biological life cycle of the local self. Instead of aging and dying, we begin a process of feeling more energy and a continuous cycle of self-transformation. Those who make the choice to evolve consciously are at the threshold of metamorphosis. We begin to trust inner guidance and rely on still unproven skills of attunement and intuition. We are challenged to dissociate with chronological age as an indicator of our vitality. Regardless of age or sex, emerging humans are preparing to give birth to an unknown part of themselves. The identity of the local self often does not fit our emergent selves, nor do we fit into the external world of the local self—its job, relationship, life style may begin to feel uncomfortable. We can experience a dark night of the soul. It can be seen as a right-of-passage. Our greater story is unfolding. We are ready to enter the life cycle of a Universal Human—a continuous process of unfolding of inner awareness into tangible form.

Stage Five: Immaculate Conception

Aligning the local self with the Essential Self cultivates a deeper awareness of our Essential Self. We become aware of a genius code within our Essential Self. We are able to conceptualize the nature or quality of genius encoded. Conceptualizing or bringing to consciousness the quality of encoded genius sparks an "Immaculate Conception." Once conceived, we desire to express and make manifest the encoded genius.

A new form of instinct pushes us out into the world in search of catalysts that will activate and access the encoded genius. The Immaculate Conception produces "essential hormones" that accentuate our intuitive sense of direction. The guidance of the Essential Self is felt more deeply. We begin to recognize our greater story unfolding out of our former life. Once the local self has made the conscious choice to evolve, the conditions for the dormant genius code to awaken are optimal. At this point there is a deepening of our awareness of the essential reality underpinning physical existence. Although we may have witnessed the nature of our encoded genius prior to this stage of personal development, its essence will not come to fruition as a viable gift, unless we are able to attune and align with guidance received from the "still small voice" of the Essential Self.

Stage Six: Vocational Arousal: Gestating the Genius Seed

Our genius seed gestates and pulses with urgency to express itself. The desire to access and express the encoded genius instinctually attracts us to others who share a similar desire to live out and express their potential. The attraction is fueled by an evolutionary urge to co-create with others as the means to self-actualize.

Co-creation replaces the nostalgic model of "I did it my way." The process of accessing and expressing one's Essential Self requires disengaging from personal agendas and ego-driven objectives. Co-creative partners coalesce around a shared vision. The local self of each co-creative partner has matured enough to focus on what wishes to be born. However, at this stage the "problem" of the local self often shows up again. We are getting ready to notice that the local self can unwittingly block the greater satisfaction of creation through ego-driven needs, addictions, and attachments. This period of attraction is called vocational arousal. It is a non-sexual attraction, evoking the essence of love. The experience of love ripens us for the birth of our Universal Human self. This is the period of gestation.

Vocational arousal heralds the advent of the birth of our Universal Human self. We may enter a season of atonement. For the forenamed the process of bringing the genius into form must be aligned and infused with our essential selves.

Stage Seven: Birthing Our Universal Human Self through the Process of Co-Creation

Birthing or manifesting our Universal Human occurs through the medium of co-creation. Once having gestated, the catalyst that releases the genius and births the Universal Human is co-creation.

The co-creative process of bringing genius into form is a unique form of testimonial that demonstrates the power of creation (when two or more unify for the purpose of manifesting expressions reflective of a shared inner or essential reality). The co-creative process demonstrates the viability and substance of each co-creative partner's genius. The fusion of genius codes expands the concept of the individual to embrace the concept of the Whole. Each level of genius is a facet of a whole essential reality. Through co-creation, each individual expands and reflects the sum of all the genius evoked by each co-creative partner. The actual co-creative project or result manifested through co-creation is secondary in significance to the unification and expansion of the collective awareness inspired by the process. What we co-create is symbolic of a "new social wineskin" that will hold the field of expanded consciousness through co-creation.

Co-creation fuses the genius codes of each partner, which infuses each partner with the other's genius. The resonant synthesis of the fused genius codes accesses the essence of each person's genius. The synchronized field of consciousness becomes a mutual resource that illuminates and expands personal levels of awareness. Co-creation sparks an alchemical process of self-transformation through the revelation of an expanded identity. The mosaic of fused genius codes reflects the whole image of which we essentially are. We are one energetic body and one resonant mind aligned and infused with the unlimited intelligence of the larger whole.

The co-creative process involves advanced levels of alignment. Each partner attunes to the other by unifying resonant templates of awareness. In doing so a one mind is formed between co-creative partners. The "group mind" is aligned with the resonant infrastructure of the One Mind of the Larger Whole. The potent mix of fused genius codes and aligned resonant templates accesses additional fields of consciousness. Fields of consciousness associated with archetypal spiritual ancestors who may enhance the co-creative process or project become available through one's resonant template of understanding.

During the co-creative process it is possible to access memories beyond personal histories. The memories encode patterns of life or ideas that are associated with legendary figures, archetypal ancestors, or past cultures. These encoded patterns are energy fields of information that become available through the fusion of genius codes and synchronized alignment of resonant templates of awareness. Co-creation taps into the same essential source of information as our ancestors accessed. There is no sense of past, present, or future; all levels of essential information are omni-present and eternal, relevant and available for accessing at any time.

Stage Seven is identified as the birth of our Universal Human self, delivered through the birthing process of co-creation.

Stage Eight: A Universal Humanity: What Is the Work for "Us" As Emergent Universal Humans

Co-creative partnerships expand personal levels of consciousness and become catalysts to self-transformation into Universal Humans. Co-creation as a way of life evokes multiple cycles of unfolding. With each unfolding, more of our encoded genius is accessed. A Universal Human considers self-transformation as one's most meaningful act. Co-creation manifests a multi-faceted, multi-essential, self-reflection of the larger whole. The sum of what is expressed reflects the dream of a Universal Humanity.

A Universal Humanity manifests heaven on earth. Co-creation will replace "the work place" by reinterpreting the meaning of work. Work becomes living out what is understood within. Entrepreneurship will be replaced by inter-vocational alignment. Inter-vocational alignment dematerializes materialistic objectives by establishing a non-material currency of exchange. The energetic exchange that occurs when two or more align at the essential level illuminates and activates untapped human intelligence. We become capable of aligning and engaging with life at the essential level. We will be able to manifest a life unencumbered by materialistic restrictions we begin to relate to matter energetically. In a Universal Humanity, our life is considered an essential contribution and not something we have to earn.

The work becomes a maturation process. The local self becomes the emissary and implementer of essential levels of awareness. The unification of the local self with the Essential Self for the purpose of re-patterning and expanding the external world weaves a new social wineskin. Universal Humans view "progress" in terms of the expansion of inner levels of awareness. This expansion will enable us to access untapped essential resources. We will be able to afford the life, which has been essentially given to us. If we live as a sacred act, we will manifest heaven on earth.

The Foundation for Conscious Evolution

The Foundation for Conscious Evolution is a 501(C3) tax-exempt educational organization founded in 1990 with a gift from Laurance S. Rockefeller. Its purpose is to educate, communicate, and apply the world view of Conscious Evolution so as to assist in the emergence of the Universal Human and a Universal Humanity, co-evolutionary with nature and co-creative with Spirit.

Located in Santa Barbara, California, the Foundation is in the process of forming the first Center for Conscious Evolution. The Center is developing a coherent set of programs, each reinforcing the other, which together form a basis for the next stage of human evolution. These programs include Education, Community, Communication, and the Peace Room.

We publish a newsletter, *Voices of Conscious Evolution*. We have a weekly radio show, "Live from the Peace Room," on the Internet, www.wisdommedia.com. We offer the Entry Course: Gateway to Our Conscious Evolution, and a variety of Intensives on Emergence and Conscious Evolution.

We invite your participation and your support in this comprehensive initiative.

For further information on our programs, materials, meditation tapes, and events, write to The Foundation for Conscious Evolution, P.O. Box 4698, Santa Barbara, CA 93140-4698. Email: fce@peaceroom.org

Website: www.peaceroom.org

Tel. 805-884-9212.

Index

Index

About the Author

Barbara Marx Hubbard is a visionary futurist, author, speaker, social architect, and spiritual pioneer. As president of The Foundation for Conscious Evolution she is developing the first Center for Conscious Evolution in Santa Barbara, California. It offers a whole-system response to a whole-system shift on planet Earth, including programs in Education, Communication, Community, and the Peace Room.

She is broadcasting "Live from the Peace Room" on Internet radio, www.wisdommedia.com, connecting up and celebrating leaders of the emerging world. The Peace Room scans for maps, connects, and communicates what is working in the world.

She is now working with a community in Santa Barbara, California, to discover what happens when a community realizes its own potential for conscious evolution. Its purpose is to develop a synergistic process in which each person has the opportunity to give his or her gift.

Emerson Institute has awarded her the first doctorate in Conscious Evolution. The Foundation for Conscious Evolution is producing an "Entry Course: Gateway to Our Conscious Evolution" on the Internet. It will connect the participants to leading books, projects, and people now transforming our world. She also is developing a variety of Intensives in Conscious Evolution, self and social.

Her five books are: *The Evolutionary Journey, The Hunger of Eve: One Woman's Odyssey Toward the Future, The Revelation: A Message of Hope for the New Millennium, Conscious Evolution: Awakening the Power of Our Social Potential,* and *Emergence: The Shift from Ego to Essence.*

One of the first evolutionary futurists, she co-founded the Committee for the Future in Washington, D.C., in the 1970s, developing the SYNCON process to bring together all sectors of society to seek common goals and match needs with resources in the light of the new potentials in all fields. In 1984, her name was placed in nomination for the Vice Presidency of the United States on the Democratic ticket, proposing a Peace Room in the office of the Vice President. She is a founding member of the World Future Society, the Association for Global New Thought, Women of Vision and Action, and the Foundation for the Future.

She is a mother of five, and a grandmother of five, and resides in Santa Barbara, California.

WALSCH

BOOKS

Visions of the Spirit

Walsch Books is an imprint of Hampton Roads Publishing Company, edited by Neale Donald Walsch and Nancy Fleming-Walsch. Our shared vision is to publish quality books that enhance and further the central messages of the Conversations with God series, in both fiction and non-fiction genres, and to provide another avenue through which the healing truths of the great wisdom traditions may be expressed in clear and accessible terms.

Hampton Roads Publishing Company

. . . for the evolving human spirit

Hampton Roads Publishing Company
publishes books on a variety of subjects,
including metaphysics, health, integrative medicine,
visionary fiction, and other related topics.

For a copy of our latest catalog, call toll-free
(800) 766-8009, or send your name and address to:

Hampton Roads Publishing Company, Inc.
1125 Stoney Ridge Road
Charlottesville, VA 22902

e-mail: hrpc@hrpub.com
www.hrpub.com